RAPHAEL

About the Author

Richard Webster is the author of more than thirty books published by Llewellyn during the past decade, as well as many others published in New Zealand and elsewhere. A resident of New Zealand, he travels extensively, giving workshops, seminars, and lectures on the topics of which he writes.

COMMUNICATING WITH
THE ARCHANGEL

RAPHAEL

FOR HEALING & CREATIVITY

Richard Webster

Llewellyn Publications
Woodbury, Minnesota

Fourth Printing, 2008

Cover design by Gavin Dayton Duffy
Cover illustration © 2004 by Neal Armstrong / Koralik & Associates
Editing by Lee Lewis
Project management by Joanna Willis
Series design by Michael Maupin

Llewellyn is a registered trademark of Llewellyn Worldwide, Ltd.

Library of Congress Cataloging-in-Publication Data
Webster, Richard
  Raphael: communicating with the Archangel for healing & creativity /
Richard Webster.
       p.   cm.
  Includes bibliographical references and index.
  ISBN 13: 978-0-7387-0649-8
  ISBN 10: 0-7387-0649-3
    1. Raphael (Archangel)—Miscellanea. 2. Spiritual healing—
Miscellanea. I. Title.

  BF1999.W4193 2005
  202'.15—dc22
                                                    2005040930

ISBN-13: 978-0-7387-0649-8

Llewellyn Publications
A Division of Llewellyn Worldwide, Ltd.
2143 Wooddale Drive, Dept. 978-0-7387-0649-8
Woodbury, MN 55125-2989, U.S.A.
www.llewellyn.com

Printed in the United States of America

The Archangels Series
by Richard Webster

Gabriel

Michael

Raphael

Uriel

Also available in Spanish

Also by Richard Webster

Amulets and Talismans for Beginners
Astral Travel for Beginners
Aura Reading for Beginners
Candle Magic for Beginners
Color Magic for Beginners
The Complete Book of Palmistry
Creative Visualization for Beginners
Dowsing for Beginners
Feng Shui for Apartment Living
Feng Shui for Beginners
Feng Shui for Love & Romance
Feng Shui for Success & Happiness
Feng Shui for the Workplace
Feng Shui in the Garden
How to Write for the New Age Market
Is Your Pet Psychic?
Magical Symbols of Love & Romance
Miracles
Numerology Magic
Omens, Oghams & Oracles
101 Feng Shui Tips for the Home
Palm Reading for Beginners
Pendulum Magic for Beginners
Playing Card Divination for Beginners
Practical Guide to Past-Life Memories
Praying With Angels
Seven Secrets to Success
Soul Mates
Spirit Guides & Angel Guardians
Success Secrets

**For a complete list of books by this author,
see www.llewellyn.com**

For my good friends
Ed and Bobbi Fowler

CONTENTS

Introduction / xi

One: Who Is Raphael? / 1

Two: Five Ways to Contact Raphael / 21

Three: How to Request Assistance / 37

Four: How to Contact Raphael Every Day / 45

Five: The Seals of Solomon / 51

Six: Healing with Raphael / 73

Seven: Raphael and Air / 87

Eight: Raphael and Crystals / 107

Nine: Raphael and the Chakras / 123

Ten: Raphael and Creativity / 139

Eleven: Conclusion / 149

Notes / 151
Suggested Reading / 159
Index / 163

Introduction

Raphael presides over the spirits of men.

—Enoch

ALTHOUGH I went to a church school, I learned little about angels until the middle 1960s when I joined the Theosophical Society. I was fortunate because one of their regular speakers was Geoffrey Hodson (1886–1983), the well-known author of many books, including *The Coming of The Angels, The Angelic Hosts* and *The Kingdom of the Gods.* He was a wonderful speaker, and I enjoyed all of his lectures.

One evening he spoke on Raphael, and I was fascinated to learn of this archangel's role in healing. My father was a surgeon, and a few months earlier had helped organize a special service at a local church to commemorate St. Luke, "the beloved physician." My father had no time for organized religion, but was involved because he was the chairman of a medical association. While my father was working on this project, he read about St. Luke and shared what he had learned with the rest of the family. Consequently, I thought St. Luke was the father of medicine, and was surprised when Geoffrey Hodson told me that Raphael was more important as far as healing was concerned than St. Luke had ever been.

This piqued my interest in Raphael, and I spent a great deal of time learning about him, before expanding my interests into the other archangels.

Before looking at archangels, and Raphael in particular, we should start by asking: what are angels? Saint Thomas Aquinas (1225–1274), often referred to as the "angelic doctor," defined them as "purely spiritual, intellectual and noncorporeal creatures, with 'substances.'"[1] Although angels are spiritual beings, they can interact with the physical world when necessary. The angel of the Lord at Christ's resurrection, for example, was able to remove the heavy rock that sealed his tomb (Matthew 28:2, Mark 16:3–4). Angels are also superhuman. In Revelation 7:1, John mentions "four angels standing on the four corners of the earth, holding the four winds of the earth." Angels possess wisdom, emotion and free will. They know the difference between good and evil (2 Samuel 14:17–20), and long to understand God's plan for humanity (1 Peter 1:10–12). They rejoice at every sinner who repents (Luke 15:10). They choose to obey the word of God (Psalms 103:20, Revelation 22:8–9). They are holy, spiritual beings who worship and serve God. Their most important role is to act as messengers between God and the human race.

Some years ago, an acquaintance told me that he did not believe in angels, but wished he did. I told him that it was possible for him to change his beliefs with a simple three-step process. Unfortunately, he was not interested in this, and I assume he is still wishing that he believed in angels.

If you, like him, would like to believe in angels but are not entirely sure that you can accept them, you need to train your mind with new ways of thinking. The three steps are: prayer, affirmations and imagination. Start by praying to God and asking for an angelic experience. If you do not like the idea of the term "God," pray to the "Universal Life Source" or any power that is greater than you. If you are in a hurry, you might like to communicate directly with Raphael, as he responds immediately.

Despite what you may have been taught as a child, it is not necessary to kneel beside your bed to pray. You can mentally say your prayers any time you wish. The best prayers are those that are spoken simply and with complete faith. Remember the words of Jesus: "What things soever ye desire, when ye pray, believe that ye receive them, and ye shall have them." (Mark 11:24) "And all things, whatsoever ye shall ask in prayer, believing, ye shall receive." (Matthew 21:22)

In your spare moments, affirm to yourself that you are open to the existence of angels. Affirmations are sayings that you repeat to yourself, over and over, until your mind accepts them as a reality. I find waiting in line much less tedious nowadays because I use that dead time to say affirmations to myself. You might like to say affirmations along these lines: "I attract angels to me." "I am constantly helped and supported by angels." "With the help of the angelic kingdom, I can do anything I choose." "I call on angels any time I need help."

In the evening, preferably while you are in bed waiting for sleep, imagine yourself communicating with angels. By doing this, you are opening yourself up to the possibility of angelic encounters.

I have seen these simple techniques help many people over the years. For some reason, they seem to work best when you use all three steps. Keep on doing this until your beliefs about angels have changed. This method works for a variety of problems that prevent people from making angelic contact. One lady I met believed that angels communicated with people in the past, but no longer did so. Shortly after using this three-step method she experienced her first communication with an angel. It was her lack of belief that had prevented this from occurring years earlier.

I have met many people over the years who say they do not believe in angels. I have probably met just as many who say they do. One of the arguments that the disbelievers put forward is that angels are minds without bodies. Consequently, it is impossible for them to exist. Another argument these people tell me is that angels came from primitive religion, but modern-day people no longer believe in things like that. One interesting point of view that I hear every now and again is that angels do not exist, as they are simply part of the intricate religious symbolism projected by the human mind. People who do not believe in God, or a higher power, obviously do not accept the existence of angels.

People who believe in angels have a completely different point of view. Many people believe in angels because they have either seen them, or have communicated with them in some other way. Others believe in angels because they are taken seriously in the Bible, the Koran, and other holy books. Others hold the philosophical view that God needs messengers, and angels are the logical way of achieving this. This was the view held by Saint Thomas Aquinas. Others, of course, have always held a belief in angels, and have never seriously thought about the subject.

Over the years, I have had countless discussions with people about angels, and eventually concluded that belief in them is a personal decision that usually comes from an inner knowingness, or a personal experience. In my case, it was a personal experience that is related in *Spirit Guides and Angel Guardians*.[2] In my mid-twenties I went through a difficult time, and my guardian angel came to my aid.

Angels are beings of pure spirit. Saint Thomas Aquinas, the angelic doctor, believed that angels were "all intellect," and consequently without matter. Meister Eckhart (c. 1260– c. 1327) wrote: "That's all an Angel is; an idea of God." The Spanish philosopher, Moses Maimonides (1138–1204), thought that angelic appearances were "figurative expressions." Emmanuel Swedenborg (1688–1772), the Swedish scientist and theologian, thought that we could see angels only through the soul, or our inner eye. The purer we are in heart, he believed, the more likely we are to see angels.

William Booth (1829–1912), the founder of the Salvation Army, was obviously pure in heart. He experienced a vision of angels surrounded in a brilliant, rainbow light.

Everyone is capable of contacting the angelic kingdom for guidance, protection and inspiration. People experience angels in different ways. Some people are able to sense their presence, others hear them, many people communicate with them in their dreams, and some get to see them.

In this book you will learn how to communicate with angels, and Archangel Raphael in particular, in a variety of ways. You do not need to wait until a crisis occurs in your life to contact the angels. They want to become part of your day-to-day life, and are waiting for you to ask them to join you.

Angels are usually pictured as particularly beautiful humans adorned with wings. The wings serve a useful purpose, as they symbolically demonstrate that angels live on a level that we mere mortals can never reach. Wings also symbolize the fact that angels can travel at the speed of thought. Medieval philosophers believed that angels did not use their wings to fly. Instead, they simply thought about where they wanted to go, and were instantly transported there. In the Old Testament, angels appear in human form, and do not appear to possess wings. However, angels have the ability to appear in any shape or form they wish, depending on the situation.

Angels bring us messages from God, and they also participate in human affairs, especially as comforters and protectors. Their main task is to praise and serve God. Unlike spirit guides, who formerly lived as humans, angels have never been human. There are a couple of known exceptions to this. The prophet Enoch is believed to have ascended to Heaven and became Metatron, chief of all the angels. Some people believe that St. Francis of Assisi also became an angel after his life on earth.

Angels are willing to help you whenever you need it. All you have to do is ask. If your cause is honest and ethical, help will come. However, you also need to make an effort yourself. You cannot sit back and expect the angelic kingdom to do your work for you.

Angels also appear unannounced in times of trouble. John Greenleaf Whittier expressed this very well when he wrote:

> With silence only as their benediction God's angels come, where, in the silence of a great affliction, the soul sits dumb.

The Venerable Bede (c. 672–735 C.E.), the Anglo-Saxon theologian, is best known today for his book *Historia ecclesiastica gentis Anglorum* ("Ecclesiastical History of the English People"). In this book he told an interesting story of an angel who came unannounced to help the poet Caedmon (fl. 658–680 C.E.). Caedmon is remembered as the first Old English Christian poet, and his hymn to creation is believed to be the most outstanding poem of its period. Sadly, only nine lines of it survive. Apparently, when he was a young man, Caedmon could not sing, and this caused him constant embarrassment and humiliation. Every evening, in his village, people would take turns to recite poetry and sing songs. Caedmon would silently creep away and walk in the hills until everyone had gone to sleep. One evening, while he was out in the hills feeling miserable, an angel appeared and told him to sing. Much to his amazement, Caedmon found that he had a good voice, and could sing after all. He returned to his village a changed man. The angel also gave him the gift to translate Scripture into vernacular poetry. Caedmon started out in life as an illiterate herdsman, but after his angelic experience gained the confidence to ultimately become a famous poet.[3]

Angels are genderless. Because angels were all created at the same time and do not die, there is no necessity for them to reproduce. You might perceive a certain angel as being female, while someone else might feel that particular angel is male. This is because you are seeing different aspects of the same angel. Angels have their male and female energies in a state of balance, and have interests that are much more important to them than sex. Gender has no meaning for them.

You can call on any angel at any time. I have met people who are hesitant to do this, saying that they are too unimportant to bother an angel. This is certainly not the case. You are a spiritual being, and your soul is undertaking a mystical journey that will ultimately lead you to your cosmic destiny. No matter who you are, you are important to God, and you should not hesitate to ask for help when you need it.

In fact, you already have a special angel who has been with you always. This is your guardian angel. Your guardian angel knows you better than you do yourself, and exists solely to protect, guide and advise you. However, your guardian angel will not usually interfere with what you are doing, unless you ask for help. This is because mishaps of various sorts can often be exactly what you need for your particular progress and development. For minor, everyday concerns, you should contact your guardian angel first.

As you know, life does not consist solely of minor problems. We all experience difficulties as we progress through life, and sometimes it is better to call on a specific angel or archangel when you experience a major problem.

Archangels are much more powerful than other angels. When they appear to people, usually the first words spoken are "Fear not." This is because the sight of them, when they appear unexpectedly, inspires fear and awe. The vibrations and energy of the archangels are also intense. Daniel lost consciousness when Archangel Gabriel first appeared to him (Daniel 8). Consequently, archangels often dampen down their vibrations before making themselves visible. They also frequently appear as people, and are only recognized later for who they really are.

Most of the time Raphael is involved with his healing work on a universal scale. However, despite his importance, he is still ready to assist you and I whenever we need it. If your problems involve honesty, creativity, education, healing, travel, wholeness or unity, you should call on Raphael for help and advice. This book will show you how to do exactly that.

One

WHO IS RAPHAEL?

Raphael is charged to heal the earth, and through him . . .
the earth furnishes an abode for man, whom he also heals.
—The Zohar

THE concept of a personal guardian angel was a popular one, even before Hermas wrote down his experiences with his angel-shepherd in about 150 C.E. His book was called *The Shepherd of Hermas*. We all have a personal guardian angel. However, humanity as a whole also has a guardian angel: Raphael. It was a belief of early Christians that it was Raphael who appeared to the shepherds by night, bringing them "good tidings of great joy, which shall be for all people."[1]

Raphael is known as the "divine physician." This is not surprising, as the name "Raphael" means "God heals," and Raphael has always been associated with healing physical, emotional and spiritual problems. There are many legends about his healing abilities. He is said to have healed Abraham after his circumcision, for instance. He also cured Jacob's dislocated hip, after he had wrestled with a dark adversary at Peniel.[2]

In Enoch 1:40, Raphael is said to be "one of the four presences, set over all the diseases and wounds of the children of men." Raphael, himself, answers the question as to who he is in Tobit (12:15), one of the books in the *Apocrypha*. He said: "I am Raphael, one of the seven holy angels, which present the prayers of the saints, and which go in and out before the glory of the Holy One."

Raphael and Tobit

The story of Tobit is a fascinating one. He was a good, upright, honest and pious man, who helped others to the best of his ability. He had a wife called Anna, and a son called Tobias. For many years the family prospered, but because Tobit remained loyal to his religious beliefs, he was threatened with death and all his possessions were taken from him. Many of the Jewish people were held captive in Ninevah, and King Sennacherib would not let the people bury their dead. However, Tobit, along with a few other brave souls, defied the king and secretly buried the corpses.

One evening when he was fifty years old, Tobit was about to sit down for dinner when he heard of another body that needed to be buried. He immediately went out and performed this task. However, as he had been defiled from handling the body, he did not return to his home, but slept outside beside a wall in his courtyard. Unfortunately, he left his face uncovered. During the night, the droppings of sparrows that were resting on the wall fell into his eyes, and when he woke up, he was totally blind. No one was able to cure him and, because he could no longer work, Anna had to earn money to support the family. Tobit felt shamed by this.

He became depressed and finally, eight years later, sent a prayer to heaven asking for death. At the same moment, another similar prayer also arrived in heaven. This one was from Sarah, the daughter of Raguel. All seven of her husbands had been killed by the demon Asmodeus before any of her marriages could be consummated.[3] God sent Raphael to answer the prayers of Tobit and Sarah.

While waiting for death, Tobit began getting his affairs in order. He asked Tobias, his only son, to travel to Media to collect some money that he was owed by Gabael, a business associate there. He asked Tobias to find someone to travel with him for safety, and said that he would pay the man for his time and work. It took Tobias a while to find someone to travel to Media with him. This was a man called Azarias, who said he was distantly related to Tobit. In fact, Azarias was Raphael in human form, but Tobias was not aware of this. Not knowing whom Azarias really was, Tobit said goodbye to his son by saying: "God, which dwelleth in heaven, prosper your journey, and the angel of God keep you company." (Tobit 5:16)

Tobias and Azarias left for Media. They camped by the Tigris River on the first night. When Tobias washed himself in the river, a huge fish appeared and seemed about to swallow Tobias whole. Raphael told him to catch it, which Tobias managed to do. When it was safely on shore, he asked Tobias to cut out the fish's heart, liver and gall. They cooked and ate the rest of the fish that night.

Tobias was curious as to why Azarias had preserved the fish's heart, liver and gall. Azarias said that a smoke made from the heart and liver would exorcise evil spirits, while the gall would restore the sight of a man with a white film in his eyes.

The pair continued their journey. When they got close to Media, Azarias said to Tobias that they should stay in the house of Raguel, and he should marry Sarah, Raguel's daughter. Tobias was understandably extremely concerned when he learned that all seven of Sarah's previous husbands had died on their wedding nights. Azarias assured him that everything would be all right. All he had to do was place some of the heart and liver from the fish on incense to create smoke. The demon would leave Sarah as soon as he smelled the smoke, and would never return.

Everything went according to plan. The demon Asmodeus fled to "the upmost parts of Egypt" as soon as he smelled the smoke, and Raphael tied him up. Everyone was delighted when Tobias and Sarah emerged from the bridal chamber the following morning. No one was more thrilled than Sarah's father, Raguel, who had got up during the night and prepared a grave for Tobias.

The wedding celebrations lasted for fourteen days, and then Tobias returned home to Ninevah with his bride, Sarah, and Azarias. Anna, Tobias' mother, asked him to anoint his father's eyes with the gall of the fish. This caused Tobit's eyes to prick. He rubbed them, the whiteness fell away, and his sight was miraculously restored. The family was overjoyed and offered Azarias half of the money they had brought back from Media.

Azarias then told them that he was actually Raphael. Tobit and Tobias fell to the ground in terror, but Raphael told them not to be afraid. He said that he had taken Tobit's prayers straight to God. He told the men to lead good, righteous lives, to praise God, and to write down what had happened. Tobit lived until he was 158 years old. Tobias and Sarah enjoyed a long and happy marriage, and had six sons. Raphael, of course, is still continuing his healing ministry.

It is not surprising that the story of Tobit and Tobias has remained so popular. It tells us that we are never alone, because we are always accompanied by an angelic companion who acts as a healing force to enable us to be the best that we are capable of being. The story also encourages us to take a risk, and have no fear of failure.

The Book of Enoch

Raphael figures several times in *The Book of Enoch*. In chapter 9, verse 1, Michael, Sariel, Raphael and Gabriel looked down on earth from heaven, and saw that it "was full of godlessness and violence." This is possibly the earliest mention of the four archangels.[4] The second angel, Sariel, is called by that name three times in *The Book of Enoch* (9:1; 10:1; 20:6). However, in virtually every other listing of the archangels, Sariel is replaced by Uriel. Sariel is not another name for Uriel, however, as in Enoch 20:2–6, both archangels are mentioned. In verse 5, Raphael is said to be "over the spirits of men."

The archangels were concerned about the behavior of the Watchers, who play a major role in *Enoch 1*. The Watchers were angels who lusted after human women. The offspring of their coupling were a race of giants known as Nephilim. The Watchers are referred to as "sons of God" in the Bible (Job 1:6). They were led by Semhazah and Aśa'el. The Watchers introduced war, cosmetics, jewelry, magic spells and astrology to the human race, effectively destroying the age of innocence.

Not surprisingly, God summoned the righteous angels to punish the Watchers. God asked Raphael to "bind Aśa'el; fetter him hand and foot and cast him into darkness; make an opening in the desert. . . and cast him in. And place upon him jagged and rough rocks, and cover him with darkness and let him abide there for all time, and cover his face that he may not see the light." (Enoch 10:4–5) Michael captured Semhazah and the others, and they were imprisoned underground for seventy generations. Gabriel arranged for the Nephilim to fight each other until none were left.

Enoch witnessed all of these happenings, and prayed to God that the Watchers be forgiven. God, however, decreed that the punishments stand. After this, Enoch was taken on a tour of all seven heavens by the archangels.

Raphael and Noah

Raphael is credited with helping Noah gain the knowledge he needed to build his ark. According to Jewish legend, Raphael also gave Noah a medical book once the flood had subsided. This is believed to have been the *Sefer Raziel*, the *Book of the Angel Raziel*.[5] This is largely a book of spells that Raziel is said to have given to Adam. Unfortunately, the book disappeared and was believed lost, until Raphael presented it to Noah.

Raphael and Solomon

Raphael also helped Solomon build the Great Temple. Apparently, Solomon was having difficulty and prayed to God for help. God gave Raphael a special ring to give Solomon. The seal on this magical ring was a pentagram, which is still one of the most important tools in ceremonial magic. As a result of this, many people consider Raphael to be the angel of magical tools and the miracles they can create. The pentagram is one of the oldest medical symbols, and this is probably because of its association with Raphael.[6] The ring enabled Solomon to command thousands of demons to work as laborers to help finish the temple.

Many ancient Jewish religious texts have survived for thousands of years. They are collectively called *Pseudepigrapha*. Frequently, a famous historical figure is said to be the author. The Books of Enoch are one example. Another is *The Testament of Solomon,* which was written in the first three centuries of the Christian Era.

This book tells how a demon named Ornias was sucking on the thumb of a small boy, causing him to lose weight and strength. Solomon prayed for help, and Michael brought him a ring that enabled him to capture all demons. This appears to be a different ring to the pentagram ring that Raphael gave to Solomon. Solomon used it to capture and interrogate Ornias. Ornias eventually summoned Beelzebub, who was also bound by the ring. Reluctantly, he agreed to bring

Solomon all of the unclean demons. Solomon interrogated the huge array of demons that appeared, learning their names, powers, astrological signs, and also the names of the angels who were strong enough to defeat them. Amongst this group was a demon called Oropel, who had the ability to give people sore throats. However, he fled whenever Raphael's name was mentioned.[7]

The Pool at Bethesda

Many people think that Raphael is the angel that entered the pond in Bethesda. In *The Gospel According to John* 5:2–4, we read:

> Now there is at Jerusalem by the sheep market a pool, which is called in the Hebrew tongue Bethesda, having five porches. In these lay a great multitude of impotent folk, of blind, halt, withered, waiting for the movement of water. For an angel went down at a certain season into the pool, and troubled the water: whosoever then first after the troubling of the water stepped in was made whole of whatsoever disease he had.

It is highly likely that this angel is Raphael. After all, his name means "God heals," and he is famous for restoring Tobit's sight.

Raphael in Literature

Raphael appears in literature as well. In John Milton's *Paradise Lost,* Raphael is sent by God to warn Adam and Eve not to disobey God. In this epic poem, Raphael is depicted as generous, kind-hearted and loving:

> The affable archangel
> Raphael; the sociable spirit that deigned
> To travel with Tobias, and secured
> His marriage with the seven times wedded maid.
> (V:220)

According to Milton, Raphael enjoyed a lengthy conversation with Adam, in which they discussed a number of topics, including life in both heaven and earth. After discussing the recent war in heaven, and whether there is life in outer space, the subject of sex came up. *Paradise Lost* differs to most accounts of the Garden of Eden, as Adam and Eve are able to make love as often as they wish, just as long as they leave the forbidden fruit of the Tree of Knowledge alone. Adam naturally asks if angels have sex. Raphael blushed, as he explained that angels enjoy spiritual sex:

> We enjoy
> In eminence, and obstacle find none
> Of membrane, joint or limb, exclusive bars.
> Easier than air with air, if spirits embrace,
> Total they mix, union of pure with pure
> Desiring. (VIII:623–628)

At the end of the conversation, Raphael told Adam to be careful of the wiles of Satan, and to keep away from the forbidden fruit. Unfortunately, his advice was ignored. However, Adam blesses Raphael before he leaves:

Since to part,
Go, heavenly guest, ethereal messenger,
Sent from whose sovereign goodness I adore!
Gentle to me and affable hath been
Thy condescension, and shall be honoured ever
With grateful memory. Thou to mankind
Be good and friendly still, and oft return!
(VIII:645)

The final part of *Paradise Lost* tells how Adam and Eve walked hand in hand out of the Garden of Eden. Despite this apparently sad ending, John Milton intended his poem to be positive. It made the point that what Adam and Eve did enables us to work for our own salvation. If we still lived in the Garden of Eden, we would not have any opportunity to exercise free will.

Raphael in Art

Raphael has been a popular figure in religious art, too. He is normally depicted as a pilgrim or traveller, wearing casual robes and sandals, and carrying a staff. Often he has a water bottle or wallet slung from his belt. Sometimes, especially when he is depicted as a guardian angel, he bears a sword. He frequently also carries a small casket or box containing the charm against evil spirits that he made from the fish that tried to devour Tobias. Because of the popularity of the story in *The Book of Tobit,* Raphael is frequently shown with Tobias and Tobit.

It is probably not surprising that the celebrated artist Raphael painted Raphael twice. In one of his most famous works Archangel Raphael is shown presenting Tobias as a child to the Virgin Mary, who has the infant Jesus in her arms. Tobias is holding a small fish.

Other artists who have painted Raphael include Botticelli, Titian, Claude Lorraine and Rembrandt. Rembrandt, in particular, seemed fascinated with the story. He painted four paintings of Tobias leaving his parents, four of Tobias being led by Raphael, one of Tobias healing his father's blindness, and two of the departure of Raphael.[8]

Raphael the Teacher and Healer

Raphael has always been associated with healing and teaching. Because he is the healing angel, he is responsible for wholeness, unity, and all forms of healing, including mental, emotional, spiritual and physical. He can heal relationships between two people just as easily as between two countries. His task is to heal the wounds of mankind. He combines both teaching and healing when he teaches us to learn from the wounds we give ourselves through our own actions. Raphael enables us to reconnect ourselves with divine love. He teaches us that we are always surrounded and enfolded by love, even when we are not aware of it.

Raphael has other important roles, also. He stands in the east and rules the air element. His day of the week is Wednesday, and his planet is Mercury.[9] He is in charge of creativity and looks after the interests of the young. He has a special interest in helping people to develop spiritually, and frequently assists people who are contemplating a pilgrimage. This is why artists frequently depict him as a traveller, complete with walking stick and drinking gourd. He is also the patron angel for various aspects of nature. In this role, he is responsible for dawn, knowledge, science, and travel. Raphael and Ramiel are the two angels of compassion. Raphael has a good sense of humor and brings laughter, lightness and joy to meetings of people.

Although Raphael is not mentioned by name in the New Testament, a Church Council in 745 C.E. approved the practice of calling on Raphael for help. Raphael used to have his own feast day on October 24, but when the church calendar was reformed in 1969, it was changed to September 29. This was originally Michael's feast day, and Gabriel's was March 24. Today, September 29 is the Feast of the Archangels.

Lost or Stolen Goods

Raphael has helped many people recover objects that have been lost or stolen. One of my students lost her watch. It had little monetary value, but she was very attached to it, as her grandmother had left it to her in her will. Diane immediately thought someone must have stolen it, but that seemed unlikely. She searched her home and her office. She delayed buying a replacement, as she desperately wanted to find her beloved watch. Finally, she decided to ask Raphael for help. Diane performed a ritual shortly before going to bed. When she woke up the following morning, she remembered exactly where her watch was.

A few weeks earlier she had visited her local swimming pool. Before going in, she'd removed her watch and placed it in the glove box of her car for safety. She went out to the garage and found her watch.

"Raphael must have put that thought in my mind," Diane told me. "There's no other explanation for me waking up with that thought the morning after communicating with him."

Learning

Raphael has a particular interest in science, but is willing to help anyone with a desire to learn. He is the planetary ruler of Mercury, the planet associated with thinking and learning. He can help you absorb the knowledge you need to know, and can also ease the stress and tension frequently associated with examinations. In this sort of situation, Raphael can help you concentrate, recall information with ease, and express your thoughts clearly and accurately.

Malcolm is an old school friend of mine. He always did well at school, but suffered enormously from stress when it came to examinations. Not surprisingly, his university days were extremely difficult, and I remember how devastated he was when he failed an important paper.

"I know the subject better than anyone," he told me. "My mind just went blank during the exam."

Malcolm resolved to do something about his problem. After exploring a number of possibilities, he decided to ask Raphael for help, and communicated with him several times. He was rather skeptical about the whole process, but could not believe how effortlessly he was able to answer the questions in his next exam.

"I had no stress at all," he told me. "In fact, I thought something was wrong. I sat down and answered all the questions. I was so relaxed, I could have been sitting at home."

Wholeness

Raphael can help restore balance and unity to your life. You should ask Raphael for help whenever anything major goes wrong in your life. Losing a job or suffering a relationship break-up are good examples. If your physical, mental, emotional and spiritual bodies feel unconnected, ask Raphael to help you restore unity and balance. Similarly, if you feel that you have lost contact with the spiritual side of your makeup, call on Raphael.

I met Donald for the first time when he attended one of my psychic development classes. It was obvious that he was carrying a great deal of sadness, but he was able to put that aside during the classes, and proved an excellent student. Gradually, over the weeks, he told me how he had been a victim of an investment scam, and as a result, had lost faith in God and humanity. This had all happened a year or so before I met him, and he had used that time to explore a variety of religious traditions in an attempt to recover his faith. Unfortunately, this had made him even more cynical.

Consequently, he was not impressed when I suggested that he contact Raphael and ask to be made whole again. In fact, it was some weeks before he even started to think seriously about doing it. One Sunday morning he asked Raphael to help him. The results were amazing, and were clearly visible to everyone in the class. Donald looked at least ten years younger than his fifty years. His slight stoop had vanished, also. He looked as if a weight had been taken off his shoulders. A smile stayed on his lips the whole time he told us about his experience, and how Raphael had simply taken away all the baggage he had been carrying.

"I was walking along a main road heading for a park," he told us. "I had a vague idea that maybe I'd sit under a tree and ask Raphael for help. However, it seems I couldn't wait that long. I was walking along the road thinking about what I might say to Raphael, when all of a sudden I knew he was with me. I'd done no exercises or rituals. All I did was think about Raphael and he came. By the time we got to the park, all my problems seemed insignificant." He smiled at the memory. "I feel better now than I did at twenty. It was a miracle cure. One minute I was in pain, angry with everyone and everything, and the next minute I was calm, free and at peace. I feel as if my life is just beginning."

Healing

Raphael is willing to help in all forms of healing, and can help restore your body, mind and soul. He can also heal the people you care about. Wounds from the past are a speciality of his. If you are in any sort of pain, ask Raphael for help. Raphael's association with the air element is useful in this regard, also. Breath is essential to life, and Raphael is as close to us as our next intake of breath. Allow his healing energies to come into you as you breathe. If you work in the health fields, in any capacity, you can call on Raphael to help you restore your patients to glowing health again. Raphael can also heal broken relationships.

Henrietta is a social worker who spends her life helping abused women and their frequently disturbed children. When she succumbed to a mysterious illness that defied diagnosis, doctors put it down to stress created by her work. Henrietta was passionate about her work, and felt that although she experienced stress at times, it was certainly not sufficient to force her into bed for days on end. She had read several books on angels, and decided to ask Raphael to help heal her.

"I didn't know the proper procedures," she told me. "So all I did was close my eyes and ask Raphael to come to my aid. I might have got the words all wrong, but Raphael could obviously feel my need for help. I told him how important my work was to me, and that I couldn't do it when I was sick. I asked him to help me heal the people I work with. And I asked him to heal me. Then an amazing peace fell over me, and I knew he was looking after me, and that everything would be all right. After he left, I slept for twelve hours. When I woke up, I was completely healed, and have not experienced any health problems since."

Emotional Healing

Natasha had many problems when I first met her. Her husband had recently died, after thirty years of marriage, and she was estranged from her two adult children. She came to see me as she felt guilty about her feelings of happiness that her marriage was over.

"I wouldn't have wished Tom dead, of course," she told me. "But he was a hard man. He put everyone down, especially me. For years, I hardly ventured an opinion on anything, as I knew he'd disagree with whatever I said and use it as a chance to ridicule me. I became a quiet, meek and mild little mouse who scurried after him, trying to make his life as smooth as possible. It must have been good for him, but it was hell for me. I felt worthless, and these feelings increased whenever I found myself thinking bad thoughts about him. And now he's dead, and I'm no happier, because now I feel guilty about being glad."

Natasha was hunched up in the chair and scarcely looked up from the floor as she told me of her sad marriage. Her husband had been equally as hard on the children as he had been on her, and they had left home as soon as they could. They had no respect for their mother as they felt she had let them down by not standing up for herself or for them.

"So now I'm all alone. I'm fifty-two years old, but I don't feel as if I've lived at all. I feel so guilty, and I'm full of regrets. I'm ashamed that I let myself be ground down into nothing. Do you think it's too late for me to start over?"

Of course, it's never to late to start again. I suggested that she write a letter to Raphael, telling him everything she had told me, and asking him to release her from all the pain, hurt and suffering that she was carrying. Natasha found putting her thoughts on paper extremely beneficial, and quickly established a close bond with Raphael. It took almost six months before she felt she was totally healed.

"I started to feel better right away," she told me. "But I kept finding more and more emotional blockages. Some of them were buried so deeply that I didn't even know they were there. Raphael was kind and patient, and told me that it would take time. He was right, and I'm glad it didn't happen all at once, as I've enjoyed the process. I've learned so much about myself, and now I'm about to start life again."

Natasha found a job, regained contact with her daughter, and has even been on a few dates.

"At the moment I don't want to get married again," she said. "But who knows? If the right person came along, and Raphael approved of him, I think I'd do it."

Addictions

In my work as a hypnotherapist, I see many people with addiction problems, such as drugs, alcohol and gambling. Much of the time, hypnosis is all that is required, but every now and again, we need to call on Raphael for help.

One good example of this was a man who came to me because of his drinking problem. Len claimed he was not an alcoholic, but drank two bottles of cheap red wine every night. Recently he had started drinking more, and felt that it was time to do something about it. Len had good reasons for stopping, and I thought a few hypnosis sessions would cure him. However, much to my surprise, they made no difference whatsoever. As this is unusual, I knew that this was a case for Raphael.

I had not mentioned angels to Len before, and was not sure how he would react. Fortunately, he was willing to do anything, so I introduced him to Raphael during the session.

Once he was hypnotized, I had Len visualize his life today, and then had him move ahead to see what his life would be like twelve months from now if he carried on in exactly the way he had been. I had him look at a few more times in the future, and then brought him back to the present.

I then asked him to visualize Raphael in his mind. I had given no suggestions as to how he should picture him, as it is better to allow people to create their own images. I found out afterward that Len visualized Raphael as a small, wiry man of about thirty, with a bushy beard. He was wearing a modern-day tracksuit and sneakers, and looked vibrantly healthy. This is completely different from the way in which I see Raphael, and shows how important it is for people to create their own pictures of him.

Once he could clearly see Raphael, I had him visualize his life twelve months from now if he accepted Raphael's help. We then progressed two and five years ahead, so he could see what his future would be like then.

When Len came out of hypnosis, he was ecstatic. He had a clear picture of Raphael in his mind, and was delighted to find out how approachable and friendly he was. The differences between the two possible future scenarios convinced Len to call on Raphael whenever he felt the need for help with his problem.

Len did not need another session. During the next twelve months, he phoned me several times to let me know how he was getting on. With Raphael's help, he had overcome his alcohol addiction, and was enjoying a happy and healthy life. His old cravings for alcohol had completely gone.

I know many people, like Henrietta, Natasha and Len, who have been helped enormously by Raphael. Raphael is willing to help you, too. All you need do is ask. In the next chapter, we will look at some of the methods you can use to make contact with Raphael.

Two

FIVE WAYS TO CONTACT RAPHAEL

L IKE all the other angels, Raphael is highly approachable, and will be delighted to communicate with you,
and to help you in any way he can. If the need is urgent, you
can simply call on him, and he will instantly be ready to
help you. Most of the time, it is best to prepare yourself for
the meeting, and conduct a ritual, as this emphasizes how
special and sacred the meeting is.

It is important to separate the meeting from your normal, everyday life. It is not a good idea, for instance, to race
home from work and immediately call on Raphael for a
conversation. It is better to come home, relax and unwind
for a while first. Later in the evening, you might exercise or
meditate, and enjoy a leisurely bath or shower, before calling
on Raphael. Enjoy a perfumed or bubble bath, if you wish.
All of this releases any stress that has built up during the

day, and means that you are refreshed and invigorated. It also gives you time to think about the different matters you want to discuss with Raphael. You might like to make some notes, or perhaps write a letter to Raphael.

You will need somewhere to hold your conversations with Raphael. You may have a sacred space, or perhaps an altar, in your home. These places are ideal. However, if you do not have a designated area, choose a room or space in which to hold the rituals. If possible, use the same place every time you make contact with the angelic kingdom. Ensure that this space is warm, comfortable and inviting.

You will need an altar to work on. This does not need to be elaborate, and your altar may be as simple as an upturned box or a card table. Place the altar so that you face Raphael's direction (east) while working on it. You can display anything you wish on your altar. You might want to have objects that relate to the four elements: a candle for the fire element, some salt for the earth element, incense for the air element, and water for the water element. If you are performing a healing ritual for someone, display a photograph of that person on your altar. Alternatively, you could write his or her name on a sheet of paper and lay that on your altar. Display anything else on your altar that is spiritual or sacred to you.

A friend of mine creates a circle of Tarot cards and conducts her rituals inside the circle. Sometimes she uses just a handful of specially chosen cards, while at other times she uses the entire deck. Another friend of mine places crystals in strategic places in her room. Raphael's favorite crystals will be discussed in chapter 8. However, you can use any crystals that appeal to you.

You can create a circle in many ways. Some people use chalk to draw a circle, or make a circle from ribbon or a selection of various objects. I like to use a circular rug. Many people mentally picture a circle that they work within. What you choose to do is up to you. You will notice your circle gaining more and more power and energy each time you use it. The circumference of the circle holds in and contains the magical energy that you build up each time you use it.

You may wish to light some candles. Use any colors that appeal to you. Remember that Raphael responds well to yellow, gold, violet, pink and green. You might also want to use a white candle to symbolize you, or anyone else involved in the ritual. You can cover your altar with a cloth, if you wish. Green is a good color to choose, as it is symbolizes both healing and Raphael. However, you can use any color that is pleasing to you. The most important part of arranging your sacred space is that it appeals to you.

Many people use incense and music in their rituals. I sometimes use incense, but find music too distracting. Again, it is a matter of personal preference. If you play music, choose it carefully and make sure that it is appropriate for what you are doing. You do not want to find yourself humming to the music while performing the ritual. Many people like to use bells or singing bowls while conducting their rituals. You should use these if you feel they will make the ritual more enjoyable for you.

You may need a compass to determine the four cardinal directions. You will be invoking all four archangels, and need to know the correct directions to face while doing this. An artist friend of mine has drawn pictures of Michael, Gabriel,

Raphael and Uriel and places these in their correct positions before starting to communicate with the angels.

Think about what you would like to wear, also. You may like to perform the ritual skyclad (naked). If you would rather wear clothes, choose comfortable, loose-fitting garments. A robe that is used solely for these occasions helps create the right mood. A green or deep pink robe would be ideal.

Starting the Ritual

You are now ready to begin. Your sacred space is prepared, and you have bathed and thought about your need to contact Raphael. If you wish, you can walk into the center of your sacred space and start immediately. I prefer to build up to that point, as a suitable entrance adds a certain solemnity to the occasion, and shows that you take it seriously.

One method I find useful in getting me into the right meditative state is to say a short prayer, or invocation, before moving into the circle. This might be the Lord's Prayer, for instance, but could just as easily be a few words that you wrote yourself. I find the famous Prayer of St. Francis particularly helpful:

Lord, make me an instrument of Your Peace.
Where there is hatred, let me sow love;
Where there is injury, pardon;
Where there is doubt, faith;
Where there is despair, hope;
Where there is darkness, light;
And where there is sadness, joy.
O Divine Master, grant that I may not so much seek

To be consoled as to console;
To be understood as to understand;
To be loved as to love;
For it is in giving that we receive;
It is in pardoning that we are pardoned;
And it is in dying that we are born to eternal light.
—St. Francis of Assisi (1182–1226)

What you choose to say is entirely up to you. After quieting your mind in this way, enter the circle. You may want to walk clockwise around the circle three times before entering. This clearly defines the magic circle that you will be working within.

Once you are inside the circle, face your altar, which means that you will be facing east. You are now going to invoke the four great archangels, each of whom is responsible for one of the Four Quarters of the Universe. Raphael is in the east and is Archangel of Air. Michael is in the south and is Archangel of Fire. Gabriel is in the west and is Archangel of Water. Uriel is in the north and is Archangel of Earth.

Extend your arms out wide, and say:

"Raphael, Great Guardian of the East, please protect and guide me throughout this ritual. In the past, I have frequently taken your divine help for granted, but I want you to know that I am grateful for everything you have ever done for me."

Keep your arms extended, and turn to face the south. This time address Michael:

"Michael, Great Guardian of the South, please protect
and guide me throughout this ritual. In the past, I
have frequently taken your divine help for granted,
but I want you to know that I am grateful to you for
providing me with courage, strength and the ability
to speak the truth."

Still with your arms outstretched, turn to face the west,
and speak to Gabriel:

"Gabriel, Great Guardian of the West, please protect
and guide me throughout this ritual. In the past I
have frequently taken your divine help for granted,
but I want you to know that I am grateful to you for
all your guidance, inspiration and purification."

Turn now to the north, and speak to Uriel.

"Uriel, Great Guardian of the North, please protect
and guide me throughout this ritual. In the past I
have frequently taken your divine help for granted,
but I want you to know that I am grateful to you for
providing me with tranquillity, peace of mind, and
the ability to give and receive."

Sit or kneel down in front of your altar. Close your eyes
and visualize yourself surrounded by the love and protection of the four archangels. Realize that you can enjoy these
feelings of love and security any time you wish.

Now it is time to have a conversation with Raphael. Start
by stating your intent. Some people like to express this in a
formal manner, but you can be reasonably casual, if you wish,

just as long as you treat Raphael, and the other archangels, with the respect they deserve.

Let's assume that you are asking Raphael to help Brenda, who is about to go into the hospital for an operation. In this instance, you might state your intent this way: "Archangel Raphael, angel of healing, I am calling upon you to provide special help and healing for my friend, Brenda, who is going into the hospital tomorrow for an operation. I am worried about her, and am calling on you to help her in any way you can. Thank you."

After saying this, pause and wait for a response. You may experience a feeling that everything will work out for the best. You might get a sense that Raphael is with you, surrounding you with love and healing energy. Whatever response you receive will bring peace and tranquillity to your mind.

Once you reach this stage, you can carry on a conversation with Raphael. You may, or may not, choose to speak out loud, and the answers will appear as thoughts in your mind. Continue the conversation for as long as you wish. When you are finished, thank Raphael once again.

Stand up, with your arms outstretched, and thank all of the archangels in turn once again, starting with Uriel in the north, followed by Gabriel, Michael and Raphael. Snuff out any candles you may have used, and step out of the circle.

It is possible that you will be successful and achieve a close connection with Raphael the very first time you perform this ritual. However, it is more likely that you will achieve mixed results. You may not be certain that you communicated with Raphael, and you may not have felt the comfort and security of being surrounded by the four archangels. Do not worry if this is the case, as the connection will grow every time you perform this ritual. After all, if you have reached this stage in life without communicating with any of the archangels, an extra week or two will not make much difference.

One of my students performed this ritual to send healing to her grandmother. She was upset at her apparent lack of success.

"How is your grandmother?" I asked.

"She's much better, thanks," my student replied. Then her mouth dropped open. "You don't think I really spoke to Raphael, do you?"

Sometimes the angels work in mysterious ways, and her petition to Raphael may have been acted on, even though she was not consciously aware that she had made the connection.

"It's a bit like a prayer, isn't it?" she asked. "When I pray, I don't expect to hear or feel anything, but I hope to have a successful outcome."

She left the class that evening with renewed confidence, and now communicates with Raphael on a regular basis. Consequently, there is no need to feel discouraged if it takes longer than you think it should. Every communication you make to the angelic kingdom will be heard, and sometimes you may have to remind yourself of that, especially when you do not receive an immediate response. You need to be patient and trust that the angels are working for you.

This first exercise is a useful one, as it activates your magic circle and brings you into contact with all four archangels. This can be extremely helpful, as sometimes you will make a request to one archangel, and then find one of the other archangels will offer to help you achieve it. In addition, this ritual can restore your soul and fill you with unlimited confidence. After all, if you have four archangels working with you, you can achieve anything.

Color Breathing

There will be times when you might be too busy to perform the magic circle ritual, or you might be away from home and unable to perform it in your sacred space. You can perform the ritual anywhere, but I must admit that I much prefer doing it in the same place every time.

The color breathing technique is a useful method that can be done anywhere. Sit down comfortably and close your eyes. Visualize yourself surrounded by a beautiful white light. Allow this white light to gradually change to a perfect, pure gold. When you can sense this clearly, take a deep breath in and inhale as much of the beautiful gold energy as you can. Hold the breath for several seconds and exhale slowly. Take another two deep breaths of the gold energy, and then allow the gold to gradually turn into the most beautiful green you have ever seen. Once this color is clear in your mind, take three deep, refreshing breaths of green energy, holding each breath for several seconds before exhaling. After this, allow the green to change back to the pure white light that you began with.

As you know, gold and green are two of Raphael's colors. You are now filled with his energy. Enjoy the feeling of the gold and green energies inside every cell of your body, and then ask Raphael to join you.

There is no need to worry about whether or not he will come. He will certainly answer your call, and you will know this by a subtle change in the energies around you. You may suddenly sense that he is with you. You may receive some thoughts from him, or even hear a voice in your ear. Once Raphael has arrived, you can continue by asking him for whatever it is you wish.

Drawing Ritual

Have you ever doodled while waiting to be connected to someone on the phone? Doodles are designs, pictures and patterns that we create while our mind is focusing on something else. At a convention I went to many years ago, the person sitting next to me filled up a whole page of his notepad with a beautiful, highly detailed drawing. He had not consciously created it. His subconscious mind produced it while he was listening to the speaker. His drawing was so beautiful that I asked if I could have it. He was happy to give it to me, and was probably puzzled that I even wanted it.

Creating doodles is a form of automatic writing. This is writing that is produced when you hold a pen over a sheet of paper, and then ignore it while you watch television, or enjoy a conversation. It takes practice to become good at it, but it is worth learning as automatic writing provides access to your subconscious mind.

You are unlikely to produce words with this ritual, but it does happen. Several of my students have produced a line or two of text to accompany their drawings.

Start by writing down your reasons for contacting Raphael. You might want healing for yourself or someone else. You may feel emotionally drained, or feel blocked in some way. I find it helpful to write down my feelings in the form of a letter, as often much more detail appears while I am composing it.

Once you know exactly what you require in the session, sit down quietly with a pad and pen. Think about your purpose in contacting Raphael while you create doodles on the pad of paper. You will probably find that some of the time you will be focused on your drawing, while at other times you'll think about your desire, and may also think about matters that are totally unrelated to your intent. This is fine. There is no need to berate yourself if you suddenly notice that you're thinking about something completely different, such as a task you need to do at work in the morning.

Carry on with your doodling until you sense that it is finished. You might experience Raphael telling you that the contact is over, or you might simply sense that it is time to stop.

Once you have stopped, stand up, stretch, and move around for a few minutes. For some reason, this ritual makes me thirsty, so I usually drink a glass of water after finishing the doodle. Allow several minutes to pass before examining what you produced. You will be surprised at what you see. You might discover a clear answer to your request, or some pictures that tell you which direction to pursue. You may also see designs that appear to have no relationship to anything. This may be the case, but you should not dismiss them out of hand. Raphael may well be speaking to you through the doodle. Put it aside for twenty-four hours and then look at it again. You might be surprised to find that things that you scarcely noticed before almost jump out of the page at you.

Be aware of the symbolism of your drawings.[1] Circles, for instance, symbolize wholeness and unity. If your doodle includes a number of distinct circles, it is a sign that you need space and freedom in which to grow and develop. Squares symbolize stability and security. If your doodle contains squares it is an indication that you are ready to create a foundation, and then build on it. Triangles are interesting, as they indicate visions and ultimate success. They show that you should follow your dreams. Your doodle will probably include a number of crosses. However, these are interpreted symbolically only when they stand on their own, rather than as an integral part of a larger picture. Crosses signify relationships, co-operation and connections with other people. Five-pointed stars are an indication that you are being protected and looked after. Even though you may not be consciously aware of it, Raphael is paying close attention to you. Spirals indicate creativity, evolution and growth. They show that you are leaving outmoded attitudes and beliefs behind, and are starting to move forward.

If you want to develop any of the above qualities, you can start your doodle by consciously drawing the relevant symbol. If, for instance, you were looking for a life partner, you would start your doodle by consciously drawing a cross. However, most of the time, you should pay no conscious attention to what you are drawing, as you do not want your mind to override the valuable insights that Raphael can place inside your doodles.

It pays to keep your doodles, as they provide a record of your contacts with Raphael. I date them and keep them in a folder. These doodles are personal. You are likely to be surprised at what you produce. Consequently, I keep them for my own benefit, and do not leave them lying around for other people to see.

Wind Ritual

Raphael is associated with the air element. Consequently, you can make contact with Raphael any time you wish by using a variety of breathing techniques. This next method is one I learned accidentally. I have always enjoyed walking, particularly in the countryside. It is a good form of exercise that allows me to fill my lungs with fresh air, while enjoying communing with nature. It gets me out of the house and away from the phone and other distractions. It is also a good time to contact the angelic realms.

One day I went for a long walk, and found myself at the top of a cliff. It was a wet and windy day and the waves were surging onto the beach below. I spread my arms out wide and took deep breaths of the strong wind, heedless of the rain that was stinging my face. The wind and rain made me feel exhilarated. It occurred to me that as Raphael was associated with the air element, this could be a good time to communicate with him. There was no one else in sight, so I shouted a message to Raphael.

"Archangel Raphael, ruler of air, thank you for giving me a small taste of your power. I want you to know how much I appreciate your hard work on my behalf. Thank you for the wholeness and unity you have brought into my life. Thank you for your gifts of creativity, abundance and healing. Thank you for all the good work you are doing throughout the world."

By the time I had finished shouting, I was aware that Raphael was with me. I could not see or hear him, but I could sense his presence. I cannot remember what else I shouted into the wind that afternoon, but I returned home feeling exhilarated, excited, happy and full of energy.

The first time I did this was by chance, but I now seek out remote, windy places where I can communicate with Raphael. The process could not be simpler. Find a suitable windy spot where you will not be interrupted, and shout out your request. I must confess that I now avoid stormy weather, as it makes sense to avoid any possibility of danger. The only physical requirement is a breeze of some sort, to represent Raphael. If you are unable to find somewhere where you will be completely alone, stand in a suitable place and mentally tell Raphael what you want to say. This will work just as well. I have communicated with Raphael on top of a hill, surrounded by busloads of tourists who were there to see the view. If any of them gave me any thought at all, they would have assumed that I was also gazing at the view.

Visualization Ritual

If you have a good imagination, you will find this a particularly good method of contacting Raphael. Sit or lie down comfortably, with your arms and legs uncrossed. Close your eyes and take several slow, deep breaths, while consciously relaxing the muscles in your body.

When you feel completely relaxed, visualize yourself in the most beautiful setting you can imagine. You might choose a place that you have visited before, or you might create a beautiful picture in your mind. It makes no difference, just as long as you feel totally relaxed.

See yourself in this beautiful scene, and then visualize a circle of pure white light descending from the heavens, surrounding you in its protective glow. You feel safe, at peace, and blissfully happy.

Now, visualize Raphael coming to see you. You can picture him in any way you wish. You might see him as a fit and virile young man, dressed in yellow or gold, wearing a hat and carrying a caduceus. In mythology, a caduceus is the staff carried by Mercury as messenger of the gods. He might hold a vial of medicine in his free hand. You might see him as a traveller, complete with staff and water bottle. You might picture him as he appeared to Tobit, with a small casket that contained the "fishy charm" against the evil spirits (Tobit vi:6–7). Perhaps you see him as a powerful angel, at least eight feet tall, with huge wings. Alternatively, you might see him with six wings, two each at the temples, shoulders and ankles. You may choose not to see him as a person, but more as a ball of yellow or golden light.

Picture yourself getting up to greet him. You might shake hands, or he might embrace you in a hug. Imagine the two of you going for a walk together, discussing everything that is on your mind. You might sit down to admire a beautiful scene while you continue the conversation. Visualize the two of you saying goodbye. You are good friends now, and the leaving is affectionate. Picture yourself in the beautiful scene after Raphael has left, and then allow yourself to slowly return to your normal, everyday world. Open your eyes, stretch, and think about your visualization for a few minutes before getting up.

When you get up, you are bound to have at least one question about the experience. Did you make the whole thing up in your imagination, or was this a genuine experience with Raphael? It might be difficult to answer this. Ask yourself if you received useful answers to your questions. If you did, the experience is valid, regardless of whether or not it was a genuine contact.

You will probably want to experiment with this method several times. This is because you might doubt the genuineness of the experience the first time or two, but these concerns will fade the more frequently you perform it. Even if you do not make a genuine contact the first time, you will gain confidence every time you repeat it, and this repetition will further encourage Raphael to join you.

Of course, once you know how to contact Raphael, you will also want to know how to ask him for assistance. That is the subject of the next chapter.

Three

HOW TO
REQUEST ASSISTANCE

R APHAEL is willing to assist you at any time. All you
need do is ask for help. However, it is much better to
tell Raphael what you need, rather than calling out for help.
Raphael is involved with communication and will understand everything you say to him, even when you find it hard
to express your thoughts and feelings as clearly as you would
wish.

Sometimes it is hard to say what you really mean, especially when you are emotionally involved in a difficult situation. Raphael will understand what you are trying to say,
and will be ready and willing to give you the healing, or
other help, that you require.

A friend of mine went through a difficult marriage break-
up. Claude had not realized that his wife was unhappy with
their relationship, and was devastated when she said she

was leaving. For several months he bemoaned his fate and blamed everyone except himself for his problems. Finally, he realized that he was at least partly to blame for the collapse of his marriage, and that continuing to hate his ex-wife was hurting him more than her. He decided to ask Raphael for healing.

Claude began by making a list of all the things he wanted Raphael to do for him. He wanted emotional healing for himself and for his ex-wife. He also wanted emotional healing for their three children. He wanted Raphael to help him let go of the past, so that he could become whole again. He also wanted Raphael to help him regain contact with the spiritual side of his nature. Finally, he wanted to send love to his ex-wife and children, and desired forgiveness for the way he had behaved.

At this stage he contacted me, as he thought he might be asking for too much.

"Shouldn't I ask for one thing at a time?" Claude asked.

I explained that the archangels wanted him to be healthy and whole, and would do anything they could to ensure that this occurred. Consequently, my friend was doing the right thing. Raphael would be only too pleased to do whatever was necessary to help my friend get his life back on track again.

I did not see Claude for almost three weeks. When I did, the change in him was incredible. The downcast expression was gone. He was bright and cheerful, and laughed several times during our conversation. He had created a ritual with all four archangels, and had asked for all the things we had previously discussed.

"The feeling of peace that came over me as soon as I'd finished the ritual was amazing," he told me. "I felt as if all my cares had been taken away from me, and I knew that everything would be all right. And then, suddenly, a floodgate inside me seemed to burst, and I cried for at least forty minutes. I hadn't cried since I was a child, and it shocked me when it happened. However, it ended just as suddenly as it began, and I immediately felt better. And it wasn't just me. The next day, several people at work commented on how good I looked."

I was delighted with the improvement in my friend's state of mind, and assured him that Raphael would be working on all his problems. In the weeks that followed, he found that he could pick up his children for their weekend visits without having an argument with his ex-wife in the process. Everything gradually became easier. He communicated with Raphael regularly. His relationship with his ex-wife and children steadily improved, and in time he found he could enjoy pleasant conversations with his ex-wife with no unpleasantness or disagreements.

Claude kept me informed on what was happening, but even so, I was surprised at what happened next. He asked Raphael to help him find a new partner. He wrote out a list of all the attributes he wanted this person to possess, and read this to all four archangels.

Three days later, he was invited to a party and met a woman he had worked with several years earlier. They met for coffee the next day, and soon became a couple. Claude was amazed at how quickly the relationship developed.

"I asked Raphael for help one day, and woke up just a few days later, madly in love with a beautiful woman who has all the qualities I was looking for. I can hardly believe it's possible."

Usually it takes time for the angels to provide you with what you ask for. However, Claude had been extremely specific. He knew exactly what he wanted and asked for it. Claude is planning to get married again, and is confident that it will work this time.

"I learned so much from my previous marriage," he told me. "I've matured. I don't think I'm anything like the person I used to be. I have the perfect woman to be my wife, and with Raphael to look after us, I think the future could not look better."

Angela is a forty-five-year-old former schoolteacher. She is currently studying to become a naturopath, and asked Raphael to help her.

"After all, he is the divine physician," she pointed out. "I find that with his help, I can learn so much faster, and retain the information much more easily than ever before. Did you know that Raphael looks after students as well as the sick? Also creativity," she added before I could reply.

"How did you ask him to help?" I asked.

Angela laughed. "It took me a while to get around to asking Raphael to help me. It was only when the papers starting getting too hard that I thought of asking him. It was easy, though. I did a meditation one evening, and then asked him to join me. When he arrived, I told him my problem and said I needed help. He agreed, and we started right away. Now, whenever I study, he is there with me. I ask him about anything I don't fully understand. He's been an enormous help to me in my study, and he's already agreed to help me with my patients when I set up my own practice."

Laurence is a sixteen-year-old high school student who called on Raphael to help him do better at school.

"I couldn't concentrate," he told me. "I'd sit in class, and the teacher would be talking, but I'd be miles away. It's a problem I've always had. People call me a dreamer, 'cause even in the middle of a conversation I'll go off into a world of my own. My sister put me on to angels. She was into all that stuff, and told me to ask Raphael for help. I thought she was mad, but eventually my bad grades got to me, so I did. I read some of her books, and then went down to the beach and called on Raphael. I didn't expect anything to happen, and was totally freaked when he came. We had a long conversation, in our minds, not out loud, and he said he'd help. I was so surprised by everything that I told no one about it. It worked, though. I was able to concentrate more at school, and did much better than before. I contacted Raphael all the time after that, and my schoolwork got better and better. I still don't know what subjects to take at college, but Raphael's helping me with that, too."

These examples show that Raphael is willing to help you whenever you need it. All you need do is contact him, explain as clearly as possible what the problem is, and what help you desire, and then leave it up to him. Raphael frequently asks questions that force you to think deeply and come up with your own answers. Here is an example.

Kirsten wanted to be an artist. Her parents worked in the advertising industry as freelance artists, and Kirsten wanted to follow the same career. However, at college, it occurred to her that although she enjoyed creating works of art, they were not giving her the satisfaction that she thought they should. She asked Raphael for help.

For several weeks, Kirsten communicated with Raphael every day. She told him everything she could about her life and her desire to be an artist. She filled her bedroom with examples of her artwork so that Raphael could see what she was creating.

Eventually, Raphael asked her why she wanted to be an artist. Kirsten found this hard to answer. After thinking about it for several minutes, she said that she had a natural aptitude for it, and that her parents were prepared to help her get established.

Raphael asked her if that was enough. "Where is the passion?" he asked. Kirsten had to agree that this was why she had asked him for help.

"I like drawing and painting," she told him. "I'm good at it, and people like what I produce. But I haven't got that special extra something. You're right, there's no passion."

"Would you be happy spending the rest of your life in advertising?"

Kirsten thought for a while, and then shook her head. "I don't think so."

"What do you want to do?" Raphael asked.

Kirsten had to admit that she had no idea. In her regular sessions with Raphael they discussed a variety of possibilities. One day she told him that she loved writing short stories, and had even written and illustrated a short book for her cousin's birthday.

"Raphael smiled," she told me. "And then a strange, tin-gling feeling went right through me. I knew I'd found what I was meant to do."

Today, Kirsten is well on the way to realizing her dream. She still works in an advertising agency two days a week. The rest of the time she writes and illustrates books for middle grade children. Her books are becoming more successful and she intends to give up her work in advertising soon. She has found her passion, and credits Raphael for this.

"Even after writing that small book for my cousin, I had-n't realized that it is what I am here to do," she told me. "It was such a surprise when Raphael pointed me in the right direction. It was right under my nose, but I hadn't seen it. Without Raphael I'd be doing okay, I guess, but it would just be a job. I'm so grateful, I thank him every day."

Because Raphael is so accessible, and so ready to help, you may be inclined to ask him about everything that occurs in your life. This is not a good idea, as you should be in charge of your own life. Communicate with Raphael regularly, and ask him for help whenever it is necessary, but do not become co-dependent. Your relationship with Raphael will grow every time you make contact. The next chapter will tell you how to contact Raphael every day.

Four

HOW TO
CONTACT RAPHAEL
EVERY DAY

A RCHANGELS are extremely busy, and spend most of their time on large-scale undertakings that are well beyond our comprehension. Consequently, it is not a good idea to summon them with insignificant problems that you can solve on your own.

Raphael is the sole exception to this general rule. As the archangel of all humanity, he looks after many areas that involve us on a daily basis, such as emotional healing, abundance, love, learning, creativity and travel. If someone is rude or unkind to you, you may need instant emotional healing. If you are experiencing difficulty in paying your bills, you should certainly call on him for abundance. If you are seeking a partner, or want to become closer to your existing partner, call on Raphael for love. If you have a new role at work, you might call on him to help you learn your new tasks. If you have a lengthy commute each day, you might want Raphael's help with the travelling. On any given day, you might need to contact him on a variety of different matters.

Consequently, it can be useful to have a small ritual that allows you to contact Raphael for a minute or two, whenever necessary. There are many ways to do this.

The easiest, and most direct method is to simply call him, by closing your eyes and saying, "Raphael, I need your help now." This method is extremely effective, but should be used only in an emergency.

The method I find most useful is to wear or carry an amulet that relates to Raphael. Whenever I need Raphael's help or guidance, I gently fondle my amulet, think of the problem, and wait for the answer to appear in my mind. Amulets are usually used to provide protection, and your Raphael amulet will protect you in this way, also.

You can use anything you wish as an amulet. The only requirement is that it must relate to Raphael in some sort of way. An attractive object that is gold, yellow, blue, green or pink would be perfect. I use a small piece of aventurine, which is a green crystal. It is regularly used in crystal healing, and I find it extremely soothing and calming to hold. One of my students uses a miniature book, as this reminds her of Raphael's role in learning and creativity. Another has a tiny feather, which reminds him of Raphael's wings and his interest in travel. Many people use quartz as an amulet to contact Raphael. This provides energy, releases stress, soothes the soul, and can also be used to contact the angelic kingdom. It makes a good choice for many people, but I prefer to use something that is more specifically associated with Raphael.

Whenever you find yourself in a difficult situation, hold, fondle or rub your amulet and think about the problem, while trying to clarify the situation in your mind. Most of the time, you will receive an answer from Raphael without having to call on him. This is because he will be aware of the situation as soon as you start handling your amulet.

However, there may be times when the need is urgent, and you feel desperate enough to summon him. In this type of situation you should fondle your amulet and say, silently or out loud: "Raphael, please come to my aid. I need your help." He will instantly be with you, ready to counsel, guide and help.

Because Raphael is so willing to help, there will be a tendency to call on him all the time. You should resist this, as you do not want to become dependent on him for help and support. You cease progressing in this incarnation when you stop trying to solve your own problems. Raphael is always ready and willing to help you, but it is a good practice to do everything you possibly can on your own before asking him for help.

You can also use your amulet to thank Raphael for everything he does for you. Fondle your amulet and send him a silent prayer of thanks. You will usually receive a positive response from him whenever you thank him in this way. You may sense his presence, or experience a feeling of comfort and security. Even if you don't, you will feel good about what you have done. Everyone, even an archangel, likes to feel appreciated. You can thank Raphael several times a day, if you wish.

Another method of contacting Raphael every day utilizes his interest in healing the earth. Whenever you see anything particularly beautiful or striking in nature, you can thank Raphael for looking after the planet. Tell him that you will do your part to make the world a better place for the present inhabitants, and also for future generations.

You might choose to do this by picking up some of the rubbish left behind by previous visitors, or by tidying up an area that has been disturbed. You will feel Raphael's presence around you as you do this, and you will also feel good about doing something positive for the environment. Imagine how different the world would be if everybody picked up a single piece of litter every time they went out. Each time you do something like that you are helping Raphael heal the planet. Once you start doing this with love and intent, you will find that you are naturally communicating with Raphael, and will realize that he is close beside you all the time.

Daily Meditation with Raphael

This pleasant meditation allows you to strengthen your connection with Raphael on a daily basis. You can do this exercise whenever you wish, and wherever you happen to be at the time. However, you will receive better results if you do it in the same place whenever possible, and at approximately the same time each day. Obviously, this will not always be possible. I like to do this meditation in my sacred space, but because I travel regularly, am not always able to do it there. When I am away from home, I usually perform this meditation in bed at night.

Lie down and make yourself comfortable. Spend a few minutes relaxing as much as possible. When you feel totally relaxed, visualize yourself surrounded and protected by pure white light. Imagine yourself as part of this white light, so that every single cell of your body is full of its healing, protective energy. Feel yourself becoming as one with this beautiful, divine energy, and become aware of your interconnectedness with all living things.

Once you reach this state, you will feel a sense of peace and tranquillity in every part of your body. Silently ask Raphael to join you, and then lie quietly, enjoying the feeling of being part of the white light.

After a minute or two, you will see Raphael in your mind's eye. In my experience, everyone seems to see him slightly differently. He might appear in robes and be framed with large wings. He might appear as a traveller and carry a large stick. You might see his face and nothing else. You may receive a strong sense that he is present, but not see anything in your mind.

Allow his powerful energy to invigorate and restore your body and soul. Thank him for everything he does for you. You may enjoy a short conversation. However, because this exercise is intended to be a regular, daily communion with Raphael, this is not a time to ask him for help. You should use one of the other rituals for that. Enjoy this brief time with Raphael. After a minute or two, he will fade into the white light and disappear.

Do not open your eyes immediately. Enjoy the tranquillity, peace and relaxation provided by the pure white light for a few more minutes. When you feel ready to finish, take a deep breath, and give an audible sigh as you exhale. Open your eyes and carry on with your day.

Communicating with Raphael every day is an excellent way of increasing your bond with him. In the next chapter we will look at the amazing power of the pentagram, a gift that Raphael gave to King Solomon.

Five

THE SEALS OF SOLOMON

ONE of the most famous stories about Raphael tells how God asked him to take a special ring to King Solomon to help him build his temple. This ring was studded with powerful magical stones, and on the seal was inscribed a pentagram that gave Solomon power over spirits.

The pentagram is a five-sided star that has been considered a symbol of good fortune and protection for at least five thousand years. Because it can be drawn in a single continuous line, it is considered to represent the interconnectedness of all things. It is sometimes called "the endless knot" because it can symbolically tie up energies beyond our normal control.

The ancient Sumerians used it as a symbol to indicate the four corners of the earth, and also heaven. They used it as a protective amulet that protected its wearers from evil influences. In magical symbolism the five points indicate the four elements, plus spirit, or the divine.

Not surprisingly, because of its association with Raphael, archangel of healing, the pentagram became a symbol of healing, and until comparatively recent times pharmacists used it when advertising their wares. The wife of King Henry IV of France had a pentagram amulet, which she wore all the time. She considered her excellent health to be a direct result of wearing it.[1]

The Greek writer, Lucian, wrote that Pythagoras and his followers placed more importance on good health than on joy or well-being. This was because the latter often followed when the person enjoyed good health. However, joy and well-being on their own cannot create good health. The Pythagoreans used the pentagram as a badge, and called it "health."[2] Pythagoras constantly exhorted his followers to maintain a good balance between their souls and bodies, and they tried to lead well-balanced, healthy lives.

The pentagram originated in Babylon and quickly spread throughout the ancient world. A frieze of a synagogue excavated at Capernaum, dating back to the third century C.E., includes both pentagrams and hexagrams.[3] Graffiti of pentagrams and hexagrams, dating back to around 200 B.C.E., have also been found in a tomb at Marissa.[4]

The pentagram was used on many Greek coins, dating from the fifth century B.C.E. to around 300 C.E. As it is unlikely that the pentagram was used on coins for decorative purposes, it was probably intended to ward off evil.

Throughout history, the pentagram has been used to ward off evil spirits, and to promote spiritual and physical health. In the Middle Ages pentagrams were painted or engraved on walls, doors, beds and other household objects to ward off misfortune. It also started appearing in Christian symbolism, as is shown by the number of pentagrams found inside churches. In this form, it symbolized the five sacred wounds of Christ.

Cornelius Agrippa of Nettesheim (1486–1535) felt that the pentagram demonstrated the harmony that exists between the Microcosm and the Macrocosm. In his *De Occulta Philosophia* he described the pentagram as revealing a perfect synthesis of the human figure.[5] Cornelius Agrippa also wrote that Antiochus was given, by revelation, a badge containing a pentagram inside four circles, which signified health.[6] He used this as a protective amulet in his successful battle against the Galatians.

Because of its close relationship to health, the Gouda Surgeon's Guild decided in 1660, the year it was founded, to use the pentagram as their emblem. Their guildhall dates back to 1699, and has been preserved as part of the Catherina-Gasthuis Municipal Museum in Gouda, Netherlands. Visitors to it are always amazed at the number of pentagrams in evidence. Everything from cushions to cupboard doors contains pentagrams.

Although he does not always get credit for it, much of this interest in pentagrams is due to Raphael and the precious ring that he delivered to Solomon. The pentagram spread around the world, and examples of it have also been found in India, China, Mexico and Peru.

The pentagram is a sign of white, or good, magic when it is shown with one point upward and two down. In this form, it is sometimes known as the "druid's foot." When two points are up and one down, it is a sign of black, or negative, magic. This symbolizes the devil's horns, and is sometimes called the "goat's foot."

The pentagram is named after the Greek word penta, which means "five." The Pythagoreans considered five an important number. Have you ever wondered why we clink glasses before drinking wine? The Pythagoreans believed that all five senses should be utilized to receive total enjoyment from anything. They could smell, taste, feel and touch wine, but they could not hear it until they started clinking their glasses.

Five was important because it was the sum of two and three, both mystical numbers. Diodorus Siculus (First C. B.C.E.) considered it important because it was "the union of the four elements with Ether."[7] It is the central number in a three-by-three magic square. David used five smooth stones to smite Goliath. Joseph gave Benjamin five suits of raiment. Joseph also presented only five of his brethren to Pharaoh. There were five wise and five foolish virgins. Jesus fed the multitude with five loaves of bread, plus two fishes. He also foretold his Passion on five occasions, and received the five wounds of Christ.

The ancient Romans burned five wax candles when a wedding was taking place. Special prayers were sent to five deities: Diana, Juno, Jupiter, Pitho and Venus. The guests were also admitted in groups of five.

In magic, the pentagram represents the universal life force controlling the elements of fire, earth, air and water. The uppermost point of the pentagram represents spirit, or the universal life force. To its left, the uppermost left point symbolizes air. The uppermost right point symbolizes water. The lower left-hand point represents earth, and the bottom right-hand point represents fire.

There are a number of magical rituals that use the pentagram. In fact, they could be considered the cornerstones of western magic, and are the most widely practiced rituals of all.

How to Protect Anything with the Pentagram

This is a simple ritual that can be done at any time to invoke Raphael's protection for any object. Start by extending the first two fingers of your dominant hand, while holding the third and fourth fingers back with the thumb. You probably created this shape to represent a gun, if you played cowboys and Indians as a child.

Draw a pentagram in the air over the object that you wish to protect. For this particular pentagram, start in the bottom right-hand point (fire) and draw up to the top (universal life force). Come down again to the bottom left-hand point (earth), up to the upper right-hand point (water), across to the upper left-hand point (air), and back down to fire again.

As you do this, visualize yourself and the object you are protecting surrounded in a pure white light. You might imagine yourself drawing the pentagram with a magnificent purple light that hovers over the item that is being protected.

The object is now protected. You can place a protective pentagram over anyone, or anything, you wish. You might like to protect family members and close friends with this technique. If they are not present, you can draw a pentagram over a photograph of them. Alternatively, you can write their names on pieces of paper and place a pentagram above them. This ensures that Raphael will look after them, wherever they may be.

An acquaintance of mine had lost contact with her teenage daughter, and had no idea where she was. Every day she placed a pentagram over a photograph of her daughter. She made a small ritual of this, and performed it at the same time every day. At the end of the ritual she always thanked Raphael for helping her in her time of need. When the daughter finally returned home, she told her mother that she had felt protected the whole time, and had thought of her mother every day at the exact moment that her mother was performing her ritual.

Averting Negativity with the Pentagram

You can also use the pentagram to eliminate any stress or negativity in your life. You need five dark blue candles for this ritual.

Start by creating a circle of protection for yourself. This should be between six and eight feet in diameter. Place the five candles inside this circle, at each point of an imaginary pentagram. Light the candles and sit at the center of your magic circle.

Visualize yourself surrounded by a pure white protective light. Imagine the candles joining together to create a large pentagram. When you have a clear sense of these in your mind, focus on whatever it is that is causing negativity in your life. See it, feel it, and experience it by reliving it in your mind. Tell yourself that you no longer need this in your life. It is holding you back, draining your energy, and preventing you from doing all the things you want to do. You may become angry or emotional while reliving these experiences. That is fine, because once you have done that, you can call on Raphael to banish the negative energies.

You do this by asking him to help you. I prefer to do this out loud, but you can do it silently if you wish. You may say something like this: "Mighty Raphael, I need healing because of the negativity that is surrounding me. Please come to my aid and eliminate the evil forces that are affecting me." Continue by telling him exactly what has occurred, and why you would like the negativity removed. Once you have done this, sit quietly for a minute or two. You may or may not receive a direct response from Raphael. He may send a message to your mind telling you that everything will be fine. Whether or not you receive a response, thank him sincerely for his help.

Finally, snuff out the candles, beginning with the one on the uppermost right-hand side (water), and continuing in a clockwise direction. The second candle to be snuffed out symbolizes fire, followed by earth, air, and the universal life force.

Sit down again in the center of your protective circle and allow the healing energies to restore your body, mind and soul. When you feel ready, get up and carry on with your day.

Most of the time, you will have to perform this ritual only once. However, if the matter is a particularly difficult one, you may have to repeat it several times.

Invoking and Banishing Pentagram Rituals

The two most important pentagram rituals are the Invoking and Banishing Rituals. The Hermetic Order of the Golden Dawn suggested that members perform the Invoking Ritual in the morning, and the Banishing Ritual at night. Of the two, the Banishing Ritual is the more important, as this banishes unwanted spiritual energy. Consequently, it is usually performed at the start and finish of a magical ceremony. Once the Banishing Ritual has been performed, the Invoking Ritual can be performed to bring down and focus spiritual energy. Both rituals are performed for protective purposes. They also remove negativity and purify the room in which they are performed.

There are several versions of these rituals that can be used. They all date back to the original rituals of the Hermetic Order of the Golden Dawn, which flourished at the end of the nineteenth century. The version explained here is more straightforward than the original, and is easy to practice.

One of the most important aspects of any ritual is the visualization. The better you can visualize, the more powerful the effect of the ritual. In this ritual, you need to visualize the four archangels in your mind's eye, as mentioned in previous chapters. Some people will see them clearly in their mind's eye. Other people will not "see" anything, but will sense their presence. Everyone is different, and the way you visualize the archangels, and the other aspects of the ritual, is right for you. One side benefit is that you will notice your powers of visualization increasing every time you perform this ritual.

Kabbalistic Cross of Light

Start the ritual by preparing your sacred space, and visualizing a circle between six and eight feet in diameter. Stand inside this circle, and imagine that it is filled with a healing, protective energy.

Face the east, and visualize a source of divine energy immediately above you. Reach as high as you can with your right hand, and draw this light down to your forehead and through your body to your feet. Do this by running your forefinger from your forehead down your body to your groin, and finish by pointing to the ground between your feet. Say out loud: "For thine is the kingdom."

Bring the divine energy up to your right shoulder, and as you touch this shoulder say: "The power." Run your hand across your chest to touch your left shoulder as you say: "And the glory."

Place both hands against your heart, and say: "For ever, and ever. Amen." This is known as the Kabbalistic Cross of Light (Figure 1).

Banishing Ritual

The Banishing Ritual is performed at the start of any magic ceremony to banish any harmful or negative energies. There are four main types of banishing pentagrams, one for each of the elements. The most basic one, which can be used for protection at any time, is related to the earth element.

To perform it, stand facing east. Reach out with your dominant hand, first two fingers extended, and indicate a spot in front of your left leg. You are now going to draw a

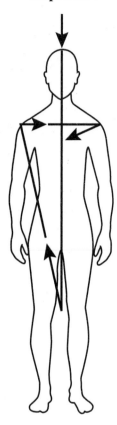

Figure 1. The Kabbalistic Cross of Light.

pentagram in the air, starting from this position. If the pentagram was a person, you would start at the left leg, then
move up to the head, and then go down to the right leg, the
left shoulder, the right shoulder and back to the left leg (Figure 2). Draw the pentagram as large as you can. As you draw
the pentagram ask Raphael for protection. Turn to the south
and draw the pentagram again, this time asking Michael for

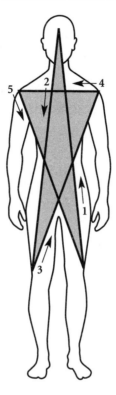

Figure 2. The banishing pentagram.

protection. Turn to the west and ask Gabriel for protection as you draw the pentagram again. Repeat with Uriel in the north, and finally turn back to the east. The Banishing Ritual is now complete and you can continue your work inside the circle of protection.

This is the simplest way to perform the Banishing Ritual. Some people prefer to draw the specific pentagram for each element, rather than draw the same pentagram each time, which is what we have just done. I have described this version after the Invoking Ritual. Experiment with both and see which you prefer.

Invoking Ritual

Still facing east, reach out with your dominant hand, first two fingers extended, to indicate a spot slightly above your head. Draw a pentagram in the air, as large as you can, starting at the top left-hand point and drawing across to the upper right-hand point. If the pentagram was a person, you would start at the left arm, then move across to the right arm, and then go to the left leg, the head, right leg and back to the left arm (Figure 3). You may have noticed that we started drawing this pentagram from the air element position. This is deliberate, as the east direction relates to air. Visualize this pentagram as a continuous ring of fire. Point to the center and say: "I draw this circle in the east, in the name of the blessed Archangel Raphael." Visualize Raphael in front of you, tall, powerful, and with huge wings. Traditionally he is depicted wearing yellow robes that symbolize the air element. Picture him as clearly as you can.

With your arm still outstretched, turn to the south and trace another pentagram, this time starting from the fire (right leg) position. Starting from the right leg, move up to the head, left leg, right arm, left arm, and back to the right leg. Point to the center and say: "I draw this circle in the south, in the name of the blessed Archangel Michael." This time, visualize Michael in front of you. Michael usually

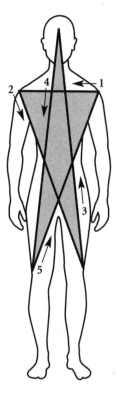

Figure 3. The invoking pentagram.

wears red robes to symbolize the fire element. He is so large that his wingtips touch those of Raphael.

Turn to the west and construct another pentagram, starting from the water (right arm) position. From the right arm, go to the left leg, head, right foot, left arm, and back to the right arm. While pointing to the center of it, say: "I draw this circle in the west, in the name of the blessed Archangel Gabriel." Picture Gabriel in your mind, and notice that her wing tips touch those of Michael. She normally wears blue robes, symbolizing the water element.

Turn to face the north and draw the final pentagram, starting from the earth (left leg) position. From the left leg, go to the right arm, left arm, right leg, head, and back to the left leg. Point to the center of this pentagram and say: "I draw this circle in the north, in the name of the blessed Archangel Uriel." Visualize Uriel as clearly as you can. He normally wears brown or green robes, symbolizing the earth element. Notice that he is as large as the other archangels, and that his wingtips touch those of both Raphael and Gabriel. The four archangels are providing a solid wall of protection all around you.

With your arm still raised, turn back to the east. Visualize yourself surrounded by a circle of flame. Spread your arms wide, and say: "Before me, Raphael. Behind me, Gabriel. On my right, Michael. On my left, Uriel. Above me, the great Father. Below me, the great Mother. Inside me, the divine essence."

Your workspace is now protected and ready for you to start your communication with Raphael. All four archangels are with you, and you can talk to any or all of them by turning to face them. You will have decided ahead of time what matters you were going to discuss, and which archangels you need to talk to.

Once you have finished doing this, you should thank the archangels for everything they do on your behalf. Once you have done that, you can finish the invocation by performing the Banishing Ritual.

Banishing Ritual Conclusion

Start with the Kabbalistic Cross, in exactly the same way that you began the invocation. Once you have done this, face Raphael in the east, and draw a large pentagram. This time it is drawn in a different way. Last time, we began at the right arm and moved down to the left foot. This time, we start at the right arm, but then go to the left arm, right foot, head, left leg and back to the right arm. Once you have done this, say: "Thank you, blessed Archangel Raphael. I now banish this circle in the east."

Turn to the south, and create another pentagram. This time you start at the right leg and go to the head, left leg, right arm, left arm, and back to the right leg. Say: "Thank you, blessed Archangel Michael. I now banish this circle in the south."

Turn to the west, and draw another pentagram, starting at the right arm, and going to the left arm, right leg, head, left leg, and back to the right arm. Say: "Thank you, blessed Archangel Gabriel. I now banish this circle in the west."

Turn to face north. Draw a final pentagram, starting at the left leg, and going to the head, right leg, left arm, right arm, and back to the left leg. Say: "Thank you, blessed Archangel Uriel. I now banish this circle in the north."

The circle is now removed. With your arms outstretched, make a complete circle in counterclockwise direction, and leave the circle.

The Star of David

There is another powerful symbol that is closely related to the pentagram. This is the Star of David, a six-pointed star, created by two overlapping equilateral triangles (Figure 4). There is much conjecture about the design on the ring that Raphael gave to King Solomon. Some people believe it contained a hexagram, while others insist that it was a pentagram. In fact, both the pentagram and hexagram have been called the Seal of Solomon at different times.

The Star of David is considered a symbol of faith in Judaism, and is the national emblem of Israel. Not surprisingly, it also appears on the Israeli flag. Prior to the fourteenth century, the Jewish people used the menorah, the seven-branched candlestick, as their symbol. However, in 1354, King Charles IV allowed the Jews of Prague to have their own flag. The people chose the six-pointed star, and ever since then it has been the symbol of Judaism.[8]

The upward pointing triangle symbolizes male energy, while the downward pointing triangle symbolizes female energy. In Hinduism the Star of David represents the joining of the yoni and linga, and is associated with the sacred marriage of Shiva and Shakti. Paleolithic and Neolithic shrines dating back several thousand years show that the letter V has always been a symbol of the Mother Goddess.[9] The V, of course, creates two sides of the female triangle.

The Star of David is considered to be a powerful amulet that protects its wearers from the evil eye. In the Middle Ages it was used as a protection against fire, dangerous weapons, and potential enemies. Because it can also be related to the

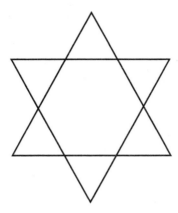

Figure 4. The Star of David.

seven known planets of the ancients, it was considered to attract good luck and prosperity in every area of life. Six planets (Moon, Mercury, Venus, Mars, Jupiter and Saturn) were assigned to the points of the star, and the Sun was placed in the center. Another positive aspect of the Star of David is that its six points represented the four cardinal directions, plus heaven and hell. In other words, it contained the entire cosmos. As a result, it is also a powerful talisman that provides its owner with awareness, knowledge, insight, inner peace and confidence. The Star of David can also be used to invoke angels.

In alchemy, it represents the union of all opposites, and is the "philosopher's stone" of spiritual transformation.[10] It gained this significance because all four elements can be related to it. The fire element is depicted as an upward-pointing triangle. The air element is also upward pointing, and has a line through it to differentiate it from fire. Water is represented by a downward-pointing triangle, as is earth, though, like air, it has a line through it. The fact that all four elements are synthesized in this one symbol is one reason why the Star of David is believed to provide divine protection for anyone who wears it. Another possible reason is that each point represents one of the days of creation.

The Star of David symbolizes the essential life-giving male and female energies in the universe. As such, it is a symbol of wholeness and unity, areas of life in which Raphael is vitally interested.

Angel Attraction Ritual

Alchemists and magicians used the Star of David in various ways to attract the angelic kingdom. This simple routine provides protection, while at the same time providing an interesting way of communicating with Raphael.

Start by creating a Star of David on the floor of the room you are using. You can do this with thread or wool, if you wish. I usually place small objects, usually crystals, at each point to represent the Star of David. (We will be discussing crystals in chapter 8.) Each side of the two triangles that make up the Star of David should be approximately seven or eight feet long.

Stand in the center of your Star of David. With your eyes open, visualize the entire area surrounded by a clear, pure, protective light. Take three deep breaths. Starting at one of the points of the symbol, turn in a clockwise direction, looking at each point in turn. Repeat this, but this time imagine the clear light swirling around with you, creating a circle of energy that goes around and around the Star of David, creating a vortex of energy. Turn around a few more times, if you wish, to ensure that the visualization is as intense as possible. However, make sure that you do not become giddy, as this will put an end to the ritual.

At this stage, you can remain standing, or you may prefer to sit, or lie down. Close your eyes, and think of the circling light that surrounds and protects you. See this as clearly as you can in your mind's eye, and then think of your reasons for contacting Raphael. You may need to ask him to join you, but it is just as likely that you'll gradually become aware of his presence. Discuss whatever you wish with Raphael. When you are finished, thank him for coming to your aid, and for his constant protection. Become aware of the swirling light again, and in your imagination, slow it down and finally stop it.

Open your eyes. Stand up again, if you are not already standing, and turn around in a counterclockwise circle, looking at each point as you do so. Thank Raphael and the divine forces for their protection, and then step out of the Star of David. The ritual is over and you can carry on with your everyday life immediately, if you wish. I prefer to spend a few minutes thinking about the ritual, and sometimes write down any insights or ideas that occurred to me while I was involved in it.

In some respects, this ritual is similar to the Seven-Crystal Ritual I discussed in *Write Your Own Magic*.[11] This is an Eastern ritual that brings good luck to whomever performs it. Six small crystals are arranged to form a Star of David, and a larger crystal is placed in the center. Each side of the triangles that make up the star is ideally seven or eight inches long. You write down whatever it is you want on the back of a photograph that shows you smiling and looking happy. This is attached to the larger crystal in the center, and the vortex of energy created by the Star of David sends your request to the heavens.

Wholeness Ritual

This ritual is similar to the previous one, except that it is performed to achieve wholeness and unity. Create a Star of David and stand inside it. Go through the first routine until you are entirely surrounded by the swirling circle of energy.

Remain standing. Call on Raphael, and when he arrives tell him that you want purification, and are performing the ritual to achieve wholeness again. Ask him to protect and help you while you are performing the ritual. Wait for his assent before continuing.

Face east and spread your arms out wide. Say out loud: "I call on all the forces of the east to bring unity and wholeness back into my life. Thank you for your help."

Turn to face south, and ask the forces of the south to help you. Repeat with the west and north. Finally, look upward and extend both arms as high in the air as you can. Say out loud: "I ask the divine forces of the universe to bring unity and wholeness back into my life. Thank you for your help."

Face east again, and thank Raphael for bringing you the healing power of God. Visualize the swirling light gradually changing to a peaceful, calming and healing green. Feel this healing energy moving into every cell of your body.

When you feel ready, finish the ritual by making a complete circle counterclockwise, thanking the divine forces for their protection as you do so. Step out of the Star of David, and spend a few minutes thinking about what has happened before continuing with your day.

Repeat this ritual as often as you wish, until you are fully restored to wholeness and unity.

One of my former students performed this ritual two or three times a week for three months before she felt completely whole again. Vanessa had been in a relationship for twelve years. She was devastated when it ended, even though she was aware that it was going nowhere.

"I felt afraid to handle life on my own," she told me. "Julian and I had always been a couple, and all our friends were couples. Suddenly, I was single again, and I couldn't cope with it."

Fortunately, Raphael was willing to help her, and Vanessa is now completely independent and leading a full life.

"I'd be interested if the right man came along," she said. "But I'm in no hurry. I'm managing very well on my own." She also thought that if she found herself in the same situation again, she would call on Raphael earlier, and put complete faith in him. "I think that's why it took me so long to let go of the past and start moving forward," she said. "I was doing the ritual regularly, but half of me didn't want it to work, because I was still living in the past. Once I decided that it was time to get going again, the ritual worked almost instantly."

These pentagram and hexagram rituals are all extremely powerful, and become even more so, the more you practice them. They also add energy to your sacred space. Make sure that you allow sufficient time for these rituals. As I like to spend a bit of time thinking about my rituals once they are over, I try to perform them when I have no immediate demands on my time afterward.

We will take our work with Raphael a step further when we look at healing in the next chapter.

Six

HEALING WITH RAPHAEL

S OME things never change. More than two thousand years ago, Plato wrote that no attempt should be made to cure the body until after the soul has been healed. He wrote this because he was concerned about the teachings of Hippocrates, who taught that there was a natural cause, and a natural remedy, for every disease. Hippocrates' approach treated the symptoms, rather than the underlying cause, and sadly, this is still what usually happens today. Plato felt that healers should use the holistic concept of treating the body, mind and soul. Fortunately, our minds constantly produce self-healing energies, but many people need additional help. This is when you should call on the angelic kingdom.

Raphael, as the archangel of healing, wants you to enjoy good health, mentally, emotionally, spiritually and physically. He, and the rest of the angelic kingdom, will quietly and gently encourage you to do whatever is necessary when you need healing.

A friend of mine was suffering from a chronic stomach ulcer. He arranged to see the family doctor, but shortly before the appointment, cancelled it and visited a doctor he had not seen before. He was unable to tell me why he had done this. All he could say was that his usual doctor did not "seem right" for this particular problem, but the other doctor did. No one had recommended the other doctor to him, but he proved to be an expert in the particular problem my friend had, and the problem was resolved. I think that an angel quietly influenced my friend and encouraged him to go to a doctor who was a specialist in his particular problem.

Another instance concerned one of my students who suffered from lower back pain. One morning, she turned on the television and saw a commercial for a product that related to her problem. She bought it and found it helped her enormously. Although this woman never turned on the television set in the mornings, she somehow chose to on this particular day, and was just in time to see a particular commercial that related to her and her needs.

Experiences of this sort, which we all have, could well be related to angelic intervention, even though we are not consciously aware of it.

Many illnesses have an emotional cause. It has been suggested that many diseases of the heart are caused by the person's inability to express his or her emotions. This constant suppression of natural energy ultimately affects the organ itself. Problems of this sort can be resolved by asking Raphael to help you understand the underlying reasons behind the illness. Once the original cause is known, you can take steps to resolve the difficulty.

Many years ago, a client of mine told me that she had worked out why she was constantly sick with minor problems.

"It's all caused by stress," she said. "And I become sick because it forces me to stop working. While I'm lying in bed, I have time to reflect on what I'm doing to myself. I think the angels forced me to rest, so that I could work it out."

Not surprisingly, once she realized this, her health improved dramatically. She began practicing stress-reduction techniques, and also began communicating with angels regularly. She found a special love and empathy for Raphael.

Naturally, if you need Raphael's help in healing of any sort, all you need do is ask. You can also ask Raphael to help heal others, when that is appropriate. Remember that all alternative healing methods should be used along with traditional medicine. You should always consult your doctor when you need medical help.

There are a number of methods of consulting Raphael for healing with which you can experiment.

Resting in His Arms

This is a visualization exercise that is extremely restorative. Almost everyone loves having a special someone to hug and hold. Even the touch of a hand can be incredibly comforting and healing. If these simple acts with another person can achieve so much, imagine how much more intense the healing and comfort will be when you hug Raphael.

When life appears to be conspiring against you, it is wonderfully therapeutic to relax into Raphael's arms, and feel his love and healing energies.

The best time to do this is in bed at night. However, you can do this exercise seated as well. Consequently, in a crisis situation, you could perform it almost anywhere.

Sit or lie down comfortably. Close your eyes, take three deep breaths and then imagine that you are snuggling down into Raphael's arms. Become aware of his soft breath. Feel the warmth of his body, and the gentle pressure of his arms and wings as he enfolds you, enveloping you with tenderness and love. You might want to communicate with him, but most of the time you will probably rest quietly in his arms, enjoying the peace, love and security that he offers.

Stay in his arms for as long as you wish. If you are doing this exercise at work, you might open your eyes after sixty seconds. If you are relaxing in his arms in bed at night, you might stay in this position until you fall asleep. You will find the sleep you receive after this exercise is highly beneficial and restorative.

You do not need to wait until you desperately need Raphael's help to perform this exercise. If you make a regular practice of relaxing into his arms, you will find your stress levels will go down, you'll feel more capable and in control, and every aspect of your life will get better and better.

Self-Healing with Raphael

It is natural to ask "why me?" when you are diagnosed with an illness. This is a typical emotional reaction to unpleasant news. It is important to go through this stage before asking Raphael for help.

Set aside some time on your own, and ask your body to help you understand why you are suffering from this particular illness. You may have to do this several times, especially if you have not previously been in tune with your body. Many people live largely in their heads, and have little understanding of the needs of their physical bodies. Take whatever time is necessary for different insights to come to you.

Once you have done this, call on Raphael using any of the methods we have previously discussed. Tell him your fears and concerns, and ask for help. Acknowledge that the illness has occurred for a reason, and that you have some ideas about what they may be. Tell him that you are willing to make any necessary changes in your life that may be required, and that you are ready and willing to learn the lessons involved.

Thank him for his interest, concern and help, and then leave the matter in his hands. Repeat this ritual as often as possible until your health has been restored.

If your condition is painful, you should contact Michael as well, and ask for strength and courage to help you until you become well again.

Aura Healing

Angels are beings of light. They are full of God's life energy and use color, light and vibration to heal us on every level. Our auras are electromagnetic fields that are made up of color, light and vibration. This means that we can ask the angelic kingdom to heal our auric field, as these are the exact energies that they are most familiar with.

Many people are able to see auras, and I believe that everyone has the potential to do this.[1] It is a useful skill to develop, as it can help you in many ways. For instance, illness often shows up in the aura before the person becomes aware of it in his or her physical body.

Your aura radiates every color of the rainbow. The size of your aura, and the intensity of the colors, depends on a variety of factors, including your health. The way in which you lead your life also shows up in the aura. Someone who is honest and caring will have a large aura, full of vivid, glowing color. A dishonest person will have a smaller aura, and the colors will appear murky. This may explain the words of Jesus when he said: "Let your light so shine before men, that they may see your good works." (Matthew 5:16)

You can bathe your aura in a rainbow of colors whenever you wish. There are two ways of doing this. The first method takes longer, but is a pleasant and extremely beneficial relaxation exercise.

Lie down comfortably, close your eyes, and take several slow deep breaths. Allow a wave of relaxation to run through your body with each exhalation. When you feel totally relaxed, imagine that you are standing at the foot of a beautiful rainbow. The colors are indescribably vivid, and you feel a sense of awe as you gaze up at this incredible sight. Take a couple of steps forward, until you are totally surrounded by the gorgeous, vibrant red color. Sense the red energy filling your body with energy and vitality. Take several deep breaths of this beautiful red.

When you feel ready, take a few more steps and enjoy the sensation of being totally surrounded by the magnificent orange energy. Allow a sense of peace and tranquillity to enter every single cell of your body as you stand in the center of the orange color. Breathe in orange energy, and feel it reaching every part of your body.

Enjoy the orange for as long as you wish, and then move on to the yellow. Experience the joy and happiness that it provides. You might feel a mental stimulation as well. Breathe in as much yellow energy as you wish, and allow the pleasure it provides to spread right through you.

Move on to the green. This is a rejuvenating color and you may experience the healing energies it provides as it envelops you. You may experience a love for all of humanity as you stand in the midst of this powerful color. Take in several deep breaths of green.

The next color is blue. Feel a sense of excitement as you enter the rays of this color. You may feel younger and ready for anything, as you enjoy the energy provided by blue. Remember to take several deep breaths of pure blue energy.

As you step into indigo, the changes are subtle. You become aware of your intuition, and the ability to do anything you set your mind on. You experience a love for home, family and the people who are close to you. Take several breaths of indigo, and allow it to fill your body.

Finally, step into the violet rays. You will immediately realize why it has always been considered a spiritual color. You might sense a closer contact with the divine, or experience a sense of overwhelming peace and love. Take several deep breaths of this remarkable energy.

Enjoy the violet ray for as long as you wish, and then finally step outside the rainbow. Visualize yourself in the most beautiful scene you can imagine. Sit down peacefully, and enjoy the pleasant feeling of relaxation throughout your body. Keep your eyes closed, and ask Raphael to join you. When he arrives, ask him to scan your aura for you, to make sure that you have obtained everything necessary from the rainbow. He may report back that your aura is looking wonderful, or he might suggest that you return to certain colors, and breathe in more of their energies. Thank Raphael for doing this for you. Spend a few moments reliving the different vibrations, energies and sensations that each color gave you. When you feel ready, open your eyes.

You will feel revitalized in mind, body and spirit after doing this exercise. In a sense, you have washed your aura with all the colors of the rainbow, and it will have expanded and be glowing as a result. Raphael has also checked it for you, and made any suggestions that were necessary. With your aura vibrant and healthy, you will feel wonderful in mind, body and spirit. You will have all the energy you need to fulfill your tasks of the day.

The second method of bathing your aura is to take deep breaths of each color in turn. Close your eyes and inhale pure red energy. Repeat with the other colors. Then ask Raphael to come and look at your aura. He may suggest you take in a few more breaths of one or more colors. Thank him before opening your eyes. I much prefer taking the time to walk through the rainbow, but this second method can be performed in a couple of minutes. Consequently, it is a useful exercise to do when you do not have enough time to perform the full rainbow exercise.

These exercises are useful as every color in your aura receives benefit. Thanks to the advice of Raphael, any depleted colors will gain extra attention to balance and harmonize your aura.

Once you become aware of the colors in your aura, and start feeling their different energies, you are likely to know as soon as any of your colors are depleted. When this happens, you can take several deep breaths of that color. You can also do this when you want to give yourself extra energy in a certain area. If you are suffering from a cold, for instance, you might want to absorb additional blue energy. If you want more confidence for a particular reason, you could inhale red to fill yourself with enthusiasm, energy and unlimited confidence.

Healing Hands

Many people have what are known as "healing hands." This means that people receive benefit from their touch. Some of these people become spiritual healers and do a great deal of wonderful work with plants, animals and people. Many people think this is a gift possessed by the fortunate few.

Fortunately, anyone can develop healing hands and use this talent to help others. Obviously, you must have a strong desire to help others, and you need to be well-balanced and stable. It is an honor to be able to send healing energy to others. It is definitely not an opportunity for an ego trip.

Start by standing outdoors or near an open window, with your feet about a foot apart. Exhale for as long as you can, until you feel that all the air has left your lungs. Breathe in deeply, consciously filling your abdomen with air. Imagine that you are inhaling pure spirit when you breathe in, and exhaling healing energy when you breathe out.

Take several deep breaths, filling your body with prana, or divine spirit. When you feel that your entire body is full of this energy, take another deep breath in. Hold your hands out in front of you, palms upward. As you exhale, imagine the pranic energy coming from the area of your heart, and spreading down each arm to the palms of your hands. Do this several times.

Place the fingers of your right hand on your left shoulder, while at the same time placing the fingers of your left hand on your right shoulder. Allow the fingers of both hands to slowly slide down your arms to your hands. Clasp your hands together.

Your hands now have all the energy that is necessary for healing. However, if you start healing without calling on a higher source, you will quickly deplete your energy and burn out. This happens to many healers.

Consequently, call on Raphael to help you with the healing. Visualize his presence around you, and seek his permission before placing your hands on the person who is seeking healing. In practice, I usually hold my hands an inch or two away from the person I am healing. By doing this, I can feel the energy leaving my palms, and my patients can feel the heat on their bodies. Experiment with both contact and non-contact healing, and see which method is better for you.

You need to send love as well as healing to your patients. Love is one of the most powerful forces in the universe, and contains every positive emotion or feeling. Love eliminates hatred, hurt, stress, frustration, anger, and any other negative emotion. All by itself, it is an amazing healer. When coupled with divine energy it is invincible.

You should perform this form of healing regularly. Several brief sessions will prove more effective than a single, lengthy session. You will find that you develop your own personal style as you practice this. Some healers chat about a variety of subjects while healing, while others remain totally silent. I like to talk with my patients, as it enables me to discover any negative attitudes that need to be corrected, along with the healing. I may do this before or during the healing. I frequently hold my left hand, palm upward, at shoulder height, to receive healing energy from Raphael, while my right hand is an inch or two away from the body of the person I am working on. I visualize the energy flowing through me while doing this. This means that I am purely a conduit, and do not lose any personal energy as a result. In fact, rather than feeling depleted, I feel stimulated and full of energy after healing others.

Realize that you are purely transferring healing energy to your patients, and that you are not the source. It is divine energy, and you should give thanks both before and after your healings for the opportunity to be of service. You should also thank Raphael for coming to your aid and allowing the healing to take place.

Absent Healing

Ideally, you should send healing only to people who request it. People become ill for a variety of reasons. Someone who is ill because it gives him or her extra attention, for instance, would not want to receive healing, because that person is happier being ill. There are likely to be times or situations when you are not able to ask permission first, and in those instances, you should ask Raphael for advice on whether or not to send healing energy. Even if sending healing energy is not a good idea, you can always send thoughts of love and comfort.

Let's assume that permission has been given. There are three ways in which the healing can be sent. You could sit down quietly, think about the person, and send healing thoughts to them. The second method assumes that you are in touch with your guardian angel. Your guardian angel is your special angel, who was appointed to you before birth and will stay with you always. Your guardian angel looks after you constantly, and will offer help when requested. He will not prevent you from making mistakes, unless you ask for advice first. Making mistakes is one of the best ways to learn. If you are in contact with your guardian angel, you can ask him to send healing messages to the sick person's guardian angel. The final method is to contact Raphael and ask him to send love and healing.

Becoming a Healer

Nothing could be more important than healing. If you feel that your life's purpose would be best expressed by healing others, you should ask Raphael to help you become the best healer that you can be. Raphael will help you find the best way for you to utilize your talents in this area. He will help you find the best modality for you, and will ensure that the right teachers and contacts arrive. With Raphael as your partner, there is no limit as to what you can achieve.

Raphael has many roles. Healing is one of the most important of these, which is why he is known as the divine physician. However, he has other tasks, also. One of these is to look after the element of air. We will look at his involvement in this in the next chapter.

Seven

RAPHAEL AND AIR

THE ancients believed that the world was created when universal energy combined the four elements of fire, earth, air and water. These elements are universal forces, and each projects its own unique qualities to the world. Over thousands of years, the elements have had numerous attributes associated with them, such as colors and shapes, and the different signs of the zodiac. Gemini, Libra and Aquarius are the three air signs. Orange and violet are the colors associated with air, and it is often depicted as a circle. Raphael is the archangel most often associated with air.

The four elements are a useful form of shorthand, and create a useful mnemonic system. Willpower is associated with fire, for instance. Intellect is associated with air, the emotions with water, and the physical body with earth. Water and earth are considered to be passive and feminine, while fire and air are regarded as being masculine and active. Unlike the other elements, air is invisible. You can't capture it, or even hold it, yet it is essential to life. It is changeable, too. Air can be still one moment, and be transformed into a raging hurricane the next.

Because Raphael is associated with air, you can contact him for help whenever you need to separate thought and emotion. He can help you eliminate stress and negative patterns of thinking.

Breath

One effective way of working with the air element is to focus on your breathing. You will have done this a number of times already in the experiments we have already covered.

Sit down comfortably, close your eyes, and focus on your breathing. Count as you do this, possibly counting to three as you inhale, holding your breath for the count of three, and then exhaling to a further count of three. Choose the right number of counts for you to breathe deeply and easily. After a few minutes of this, you will find yourself drifting into a contemplative, meditative state.

Think about the element of air, and what it means to you. Recall times when air invigorated or excited you. You might remember flying a kite in windy weather when you were a child. I remember laughing with joy as I ran into a powerful wind when I was three or four years old.

Think about Raphael and what you already know about him. Think about his association with the air element, and see how this relates to his other areas of interest, such as creativity, communication, learning, love, and having a good time. You might want to contact him at this time, or you may simply send him a message of thanks.

Focus on your breathing again for a few breaths, and then open your eyes. Pausing in your daily routine to take several slow, deep breaths is a good way of reducing stress and tension. It also reminds you that Raphael's influence totally surrounds you, all the time.

Healing with Your Breath

Healing by breathing on a wound or afflicted part of the body is an extremely old practice, and one that can be used as an adjunct to other healing methods. Before you start, take several slow deep breaths to fill your body with healing energy. I like to visualize myself inhaling a pure green color, as this color is associated with healing. When you feel that your body is full of healing energy, lean close to the afflicted part of your body and blow gently on the wound, visualizing it becoming whole and perfect again. Do this for two or three minutes, twice a day, until the wound is healed.

You can also use this technique, known as insufflation, to infuse anything you are working on with beneficial energy. An acquaintance of mine who writes steamy romance novels always blows red energy on to her pages before starting to write. She says this helps her get into the correct frame of mind to write the types of books that her audience wants.

Incense

Smoke is another way of making the air element visible. As the swirling smoke spirals and ascends skyward, we gain a sense of the mysterious and mystical qualities of air. People have used incense in rites and rituals for thousands of years to represent the air element, and also to affect changes in awareness. Originally, the sweet smell of burning incense was believed to attract the attention of the gods. People also believed that prayers and petitions would be carried up to heaven on the sweet-smelling smoke. There are a number of references to this in the Bible.[1] The first known recipe for incense also appears in the Bible (Exodus 30:34). However, the Hebrews were not the first people to use incense for these purposes. It seems likely that they learned it from the Sumerians, Babylonians, Chaldeans, Canaanites and Egyptians. In ancient Egypt, incense-making was considered such an important art that only specialized, highly trained priests were allowed to manufacture it. Frankincense was burned at sunrise, myrrh at noon, and kyphi at sunset to celebrate the progress of the Sun God Ra as he went through a day.

Incense was used at Delphi. The Oracle would be surrounded by smoke, and this helped her enter the necessary trance state to make her predictions. Although no one knows exactly what was burned at Delphi, people have suggested both datura leaves and laurel. These would certainly create the right altered state.

Incense can be purchased for many purposes. Here are some suggested herbs that can be used to create incense for a variety of different goals:

Cleansing of Sacred Space—Cinnamon, Clove, Pine, Thyme, Vervain.

Confidence—Fennel, Garlic, Musk, Oak, Rosemary, St. John's Wort, Tarragon, Thyme, Turmeric.

Divination—Anise, Althea, Basil, Cassia, Cedar, Cinnamon, Cinquefoil, Coriander, Frankincense, Lavender, Lilac, Mugwort, Rose, St. John's Wort, Sandalwood, Thyme, Valerian, Wormwood, Yarrow, Yew.

Pleasant Dreams and Protection While Asleep—Camomile, Catnip, Jasmine, Lemon Verbena, Marigold, Mugwort, Nutmeg, Peppermint, Primrose, Spearmint, Sunflower.

Healing—Aloe, Ash, Camomile, Cinnamon, Eucalyptus, Fennel, Garlic, Marjoram, Mint, Nettle, Onion, Pine, Rosemary, Rowan, Saffron, Sage, Sandalwood, Thyme, Willow, Yarrow.

Intuition—Bay Laurel, Bay Leaves, Cinnamon, Cowslip, Elder, Eyebright, Hazel, Hyssop, Lavender, Marigold, Mugwort, Nutmeg, Oak, Rose, Thyme, Wormwood, Yarrow.

Love—Allspice, Ambergris, Angelica, Anise, Balm of Gilead, Basil, Bergamot, Cassia, Cherry, Cinnamon, Cinquefoil, Cloves, Coriander, Dill, Dragon's Blood, Elder, Fennel, Ginger, Ginseng, Honeysuckle, Jasmine, Lavender, Lemon Balm, Lilac, Mandrake, Marigold, Marjoram, Meadowsweet, Mistletoe, Motherwort, Musk, Myrtle, Orange, Orchid, Oregano, Orris,

Peppermint, Plantain, Primrose, Rose, Rosemary, Sage, Sandalwood, Spearmint, Tarragon, Thyme, Valerian, Vetiver, Violet, Wisteria, Wormwood, Yarrow.

Meditation—Acacia, Camomile, Frankincense, Jasmine, Parsley, Sage, Sandalwood, Thyme, Vervain.

Peace—Aloe, Camomile, Gardenia, Lavender, Violet.

Prosperity—Agrimony, Anise, Camomile, Cassia, Cinnamon, Clover, Dandelion, Dragon's Blood, Frankincense, Honeysuckle, Lavender, Linden, Marigold, Meadowsweet, Mistletoe, Musk, Myrrh, Nutmeg, Orange, Peppermint, Rose, Rosemary, St. John's Wort, Sandalwood, Spearmint, Solomon's Seal, Sunflower, Vetiver, Wintergreen, Yarrow.

Protection—Acacia, Aloe, Angelica, Anise, Balm of Gilead, Basil, Betony, Caraway, Camomile, Cassia, Cinnamon, Cinquefoil, Clove, Coriander, Dill, Dragon's Blood, Fennel, Fern, Garlic, Hawthorn, Holly, Hyssop, Ivy, Lavender, Lemon Verbena, Lilac, Mandrake, Marjoram, Meadowsweet, Mugwort, Onion, Periwinkle, Rose, Rosemary, Rowan, Sage, St. John's Wort, Sandalwood, Vervain, Witch Hazel, Wormwood.

Purification—Anise, Benzoin, Betony, Cinquefoil, Dragon's Blood, Fennel, Frankincense, Hyssop, Lavender, Lemon, Pine, Rosemary, Sandalwood, Thyme, Valerian, Vervain.

Raphael—Aniseed, Basil, Cassia, Cinnamon, Cloves, Dammar, Dill, Eyebright, Hazel, Lemon Verbena,

Lilac, Lime, Marjoram, Mint, Nutmeg, Peppermint, Sandalwood, Storax, Vervain.

Spirituality—Cinnamon, Clover, Frankincense, Myrrh, Sandalwood.

Success—Angelica, Basil, Cedar, Cinnamon, Frankincense, Ginger, Heather, Lemon Balm, Lemon Verbena, Marigold, Mistletoe, Myrrh, Rose, Rowan, St. John's Wort, Solomon's Seal.

Wisdom and Knowledge—Angelica, Balm of Gilead, Basil, Cassia, Cinnamon, Garlic, Rosemary, Sage, Solomon's Seal, Sunflower, Thyme, Wormwood, Yarrow.

There are a number of books available that can teach you how to make your own incense.[2] Alternatively, you may prefer to buy it. Cone and stick incense can be bought for a wide range of purposes, and are readily available.

You may wish to burn incense while meditating, or when contacting Raphael. You can pass objects through the smoke of an appropriate incense to imbue them with the qualities that you desire. If you wanted more money, for instance, you could pass a small object that related to this purpose through the smoke produced by a prosperity incense to create a powerful talisman that would draw abundance to it. You can also use incense to eliminate unwanted energies. Use a strong or fiery incense for this, and visualize it carrying away unwanted attitudes or beliefs. Once you have done this, you should then burn another incense that contains the qualities you want to encourage. Naturally, you can burn incense at any time. This will remind you that Raphael is always close and will, at the same time, allow you to reap the additional benefits that the particular incense offers.

Potpourri Pot

Not everyone likes incense, and a potpourri pot makes an effective substitute. It is a small pot that sits on a frame above a candle. Potpourri pots are readily available at gift and import stores. Place some water in the pot, and add some herbs. Light the candle, and wait for the water to slowly evaporate, filling the air with a delicate fragrance. This, incidentally, creates perfect conditions for any work involving Raphael because all four elements are involved. Water comes from the pot, fire from the candle, earth from the herbs, and air is produced as the water evaporates. Three elements combine to produce Raphael's element of air.

Voice and Sound

"In the beginning was the Word." (John 1:1) This quote shows that in the Judeo-Christian tradition, the Word was synonymous with the act of creation, and that words can create. Words have always been considered powerful, as the famous Hebrew story of the golem shows. A rabbi made a man out of clay, and gave him life by writing a sacred name on his forehead. Unfortunately, the golem went out of control. The rabbi changed one letter of the sacred name, so that it now read "death." The golem immediately died.

In the Muslim tradition, Muhammad heard a voice while meditating in a cave. This voice told him that he would become the religious leader of his people. Over a period of time, this voice dictated the Koran to him. Muslims believe that this voice was that of Archangel Gabriel.

Sound is energy, and the spoken word sends vibrating energy through Raphael's element of air. This means that your voice is an effective tool that enhances all communication with Raphael. Obviously, your voice is connected with the air element, and your words are potentially unbelievably powerful. Every time you speak you send your message through the air. You can use this to gain a closer relationship with Raphael.

Chanting is a powerful way to create psychic and spiritual energy. It has also been used by many religions as a way of achieving an altered state of awareness. In fact, this is where the word enchantment comes from. Someone or something becomes enchanted by the chant. Hebrew mystics use the secret names of God, for instance, while followers of Islam chant the ninety-nine names of Allah. Mantras are commonly chanted in the East. Om (or aum) is considered to be the voice of the universe.

I enjoy listening to CDs of Gregorian chant, and regularly play them to others so they can understand what chanting is actually about. This also helps them understand the technique. Listening to chanting is therapeutic and enjoyable, but you experience much, much more when you participate.

Toning is an effective technique of producing sounds without words. Everything in the universe has its own special note. Knowledge of this allows toners to heal others by producing the correct note for the people they are dealing with.

Every sound you make is received by the air element. Consequently, every time you sing or hum you are sending a message to Raphael. These are likely to be positive messages, as most people sing only when they are feeling happy. Drumming, clapping of hands, and playing a musical instrument have the same effect.

The expression "music of the spheres" relates to the heavenly sounds heard by holy people while in a state of trance or ecstasy. In the Bible, we read:

> After this I looked, and, behold, a door was opened in heaven: and the first voice which I heard was as it were of a trumpet talking with me; which said, Come up hither, and I will shew thee things which must be hereafter. (Revelation 4:1)

Naturally, the music of the spheres also includes the sounds of angels: "And I beheld, and I heard the voice of many angels about the throne." (Revelation 5:11) Angels are often depicted playing harps. This tradition could well have come about as a result of people hearing them play.

Not long ago, I was speaking to a piano teacher who told me that she regularly caught a glimpse of an angel when one of her pupils played the piano. She wanted to know why she saw the angel only when this particular student played. She also thought she might be imagining the whole experience. The angelic appearance was real. Over the years, I have spoken to many people who have seen angels when beautiful music was being played. I also think that the reason she saw angels when this student played was because he totally lost himself in the music. In effect, he was sending a prayer to heaven every time he played.

Saying prayers out loud also uses your voice. It may not be possible to do this all the time, but it can be an uplifting experience to do this. Many people have reported feeling a closer connection with the divine when they have expressed their prayers out loud.

There are many misconceptions about prayers. You can pray anywhere, at any time. A prayer is a conversation with the architect of the universe. It may sometimes feel like a one-way conversation, and this is not surprising when you think that most people pray only when they want something. Your prayers should include thanks for the blessings in your life, and for all the opportunities you have to grow and develop. You should speak normally, also. There is no need to say your prayers in a highly formal, stilted manner.

In Tibet many people use prayer wheels and prayer flags. Both of these use the air element. The mantras written on the flags are blown into the universe by the wind. Mantras are also written on rolls of paper that are consecrated by a lama and placed inside a prayer wheel. This wheel is then turned, bringing the air element into play. Turning the wheel is not considered as effective as saying the words out loud. Consequently, it needs to be repeated many more times to make it as effective. Mantras are believed to possess potent energy, but because they are difficult to master, most Tibetans prefer to use the prayer flags and prayer wheels.

Wind chimes can be a useful addition to the home, as they regularly remind you of Raphael and the element of air.

Glossolalia

Glossolalia means "speaking in tongues." It normally occurs when the speaker is in a heightened state of awareness, and he or she is not usually aware of what is going on. Because it uses the voice, this phenomenon is connected with Raphael, and you can use glossolalia to receive messages from the angelic kingdom. However, as you may not be aware of what has occurred, it pays to have someone with you to record the session, or to take notes.

Sit or kneel in your sacred space, close your eyes, and relax. In your mind's eye, see yourself existing on several different planes at the same time. Think of your physical body that keeps you grounded to the earth. Direct your attention to your mental body that allows you to think and create. You have an emotional body that allows you to feel. Your intuitive body allows you to sense, and your spiritual body is an integral part of the divine.

As you think about this, become aware of each of these bodies, and realize just how special you are. You can achieve anything you want, and now your goal is to communicate with Raphael.

Start singing the name Raphael, using a different note for each syllable. Pronounce it: Raf - ay - el. Keep on singing the same three notes over and over again. You will notice the sounds reverberating throughout your body as you do this, stimulating and revitalizing every single cell. Many people become unexpectedly emotional as they do this. This is perfectly natural, and there is no need to be concerned if this occurs.

After a while, you will become aware that you have moved into an altered state. By now, you should almost be unaware of the fact that you are still singing the same three notes over and over again. Suddenly, you will stop singing, and will start talking in a strange tongue. You are unlikely to be aware of this yourself. It will stop as suddenly as it began, and you will become aware of yourself again.

Take a few slow, deep breaths to center yourself, and then open your eyes. Although you may not consciously be aware of what happened, you will find yourself full of spiritual energy. This is a gift from Raphael. Spread your arms, and thank him sincerely for his blessing upon you. When you feel ready, get up and carry on with your day.

Affirmations

Affirmations are positive suggestions that are deliberately implanted into the subconscious mind to achieve certain goals. They consist of short sayings that are repeated over and over again until the subconscious mind accepts them as fact. Once this occurs, the person's conscious mind will start acting on them and the beneficial changes will take place automatically.

Affirmations show how important it is to think positively. As we go through life we pick up attitudes and beliefs from others, and frequently these hold us back later on. If your parents had a negative attitude toward money, for instance, you are likely to have the same feelings about money that they had. This means that you are subconsciously sabotaging yourself. The remedy is to change your beliefs about money.

We all have some fifty to sixty thousand thoughts a day, and most of the time we have no idea how many thoughts are positive and how many negative. Affirmations enable us to take control and insert positive thoughts into our minds.

You can repeat your affirmations silently or out loud. It is better to say them out loud, whenever possible, as this involves the air element, and also enables you to hear them, bringing another sense into the process. Obviously, this is not always possible. I regularly say affirmations to myself while waiting in line at the bank or supermarket. On these occasions, I repeat them to myself silently.

Affirmations should be phrased in the present tense, as if you already possess whatever it is you are seeking. Here are some affirmations that I have found helpful:

"I am in tune with the universe."

"I enjoy a close, loving relationship with Raphael."

"I am a loving and caring person."

"I experience abundance in every area of my life."

It is important that you feel comfortable with your affirmations. If you do not believe that you could ever experience abundance in every area of your life, you will send that thought into your subconscious along with the affirmation, and it will not work until you change your fundamental beliefs.

If you are unsure about any affirmation, repeat it to yourself several times, while listening to see what your body is telling you about it. You may feel a sense of discomfort, such as a tightening in your chest or a lump in your throat. This is your body's way of telling you that it is unhappy with the affirmation. Spend some time thinking about why this might be the case, and then say the affirmation again. Keep on doing this until your body gives no response or responds favorably. Once you reach this point, you will be able to say the affirmation, and know that it is being acted on by your subconscious mind.

You should repeat your affirmations as frequently as possible. Experiment by singing them, as well as saying them. Put the emphasis on different words. Whisper them and shout them. Enjoy the process, and remember that Raphael is aware of what you are doing, and will play an active role in helping you to achieve your goals.

You can invite Raphael to join you while you say your affirmations, if you wish. Relax in your sacred space, and when you feel ready, ask Raphael to join you. Tell him what you are planning to do. Explain each affirmation, and the reason why you are saying it. Tell him what changes you intend to make in your life, and ask him for his help in making them a reality.

After doing this, close your eyes and say your affirmations with as much energy and enthusiasm as possible. Feel the effect each affirmation is having on you as you say it. Sing some of them, say some in funny voices, emphasize different words, and chant some of them. By the time you have finished doing this, you will feel totally revitalized and feel that you are capable of achieving anything.

When you have finished, ask Raphael for his input. Whatever he suggests will be helpful. He might think that you are doing an excellent job and should carry on the way you are. He might suggest you change the wording of a particular affirmation. He may suggest you eliminate one affirmation and replace it with another.

Discuss anything you wish with Raphael, and then thank him. Obviously, you will not be able to do this every time you do your affirmations, but you will notice that your progress is smoother and easier when Raphael is actively involved.

Do not expect immediate results with your affirmations. You are planting seeds in your subconscious mind and you need to keep repeating them over and over again. In time, they will be accepted by your subconscious mind, and you will find yourself leading the life that you always dreamed about.

Mantra Meditation

Mantras are sacred words taken from the ancient Vedic scriptures. The person reciting these phrases is filled with their power and intent. This happens in a variety of ways. First of all, the literal meaning of the phrase is accepted by the person reciting it. The vibrations created in the body while the mantra is being recited have a profound effect on the person's physical, mental, emotional and spiritual state. Finally, of course, there is the magical element. This is the intent behind every mantra.

Om mani padme hum is the best known mantra in the West. The literal translation of this is: "O, thou jewel of the lotus." However, it means much more than that. Mani means anything precious, which includes an enlightened mind. Padme represents the lotus blossom, but more importantly, it also indicates a spiritual awakening. Om represents the universal cosmic consciousness. This means that body, mind and spirit are all represented in this one mantra. In the Buddhist tradition the lotus (padma) signifies our own heart, and living in it is the jewel (mani), namely Buddha. In Singapore this mantra means "May there be peace in the world."

Om is pronounced aum. Because this word starts in the deepest part of the throat and ends with the lips closed, it relates to alpha and omega, the beginning and the end. Mani is pronounced mah-nee, padme is pronounced pahd-may, and hum is haum. You say this mantra by taking a long deep breath. Om is said during the first half of the exhalation, followed by mani padme, and a lengthy hum at the end.

You should feel a powerful vibration, almost like a hum, pass over you as you say this mantra. As you repeat it, again and again, you will gradually feel yourself becoming in touch with the infinite. This is the purpose of mantras. You gain a sense of peace and contentment, while, at the same time, gradually become closer and closer to the universal life force.

Om mani padme hum can be used for virtually any purpose, but there are numerous mantras that are intended for specific goals.[3] Mantras work because the vibrations of the sounds on the nervous system cause beneficial effects on the person who is reciting them.

In India, each mantra has to be recited a certain number of times. People use strings of beads, similar to rosary beads, to help them do this. Each string contains 108 beads, one of which is slightly larger than the others. This bead is known as the Guru bead. As this bead can never be crossed, the person reciting the mantra stops after 108 repetitions, or starts going back in the other direction.

I have been asked how reciting an Eastern mantra, such as *Om mani padme hum*, can help a Westerner gain a closer connection with Raphael. Apart from the fact that Raphael is willing to help anyone, no matter where in the world they may live, or what their background is, mantras use the element of air. Consequently, no matter whether you say an affirmation, prayer, or mantra, Raphael will hear it.

Sound plays an important role in many spiritual disciplines. Nada yoga, for instance, is sound meditation, and uses mantras to focus the mind.

How to Send Written Messages to Raphael

In *Write Your Own Magic* I mentioned an elderly man who wrote his requests on paper with invisible ink, and then sent them into the air from the top of a sacred mountain.[4] I had a conversation with him once I noticed that he sent his darts off in the four cardinal directions. He also mumbled some words to himself as he sent them into flight. I had played with invisible ink as a child, but it had never occurred to me to use it when sending messages to the angelic kingdom. Obviously, I would not want other people to read my messages to Raphael, and the more I thought about it, the more logical it became.

I experimented in a park near my home. I wrote three messages, using different forms of invisible ink for each one. I used milk for one, lemon juice for another, and a commercially made invisible ink for the third. I then turned the sheets of paper into darts, and went to the park early one Wednesday morning. I faced east and, just as dawn broke, I sent the darts into the air with a brief blessing. By now you will know why I chose the day, time and direction. Wednesday is the day of Mercury, which is related to Raphael. Dawn is the time of day that is related to the air element. East is Raphael's direction. I felt this gave my petitions the best possible start.

I was standing on a small mound, and the darts were immediately caught by a gentle breeze and soared and danced for a while before landing on the grass. Two darts landed about a hundred yards away from me, but the third travelled for more than three hundred yards, and stopped only when caught by a hedge.

I was excited about sending my messages to Raphael in this way, but immediately had a new problem. Should I leave the darts where they had landed, or should I pick them up and place them in a trash can? I dislike leaving rubbish lying around, and usually try to leave the places I visit in a better condition than they were when I arrived.

I compromised by picking up the darts and taking them home with me. My requests to Raphael concerned a creative project I was working on that had proven to be far more difficult than expected. I almost forgot about this request, as I was busy with a variety of projects. One evening, a few weeks later, I noticed the darts sitting on a shelf in my office. I immediately realized that I had finished the project that had been causing me difficulty. The work had gone so smoothly after sending my message to Raphael that I had completely forgotten how difficult it had been. I immediately sent a message of thanks to Raphael.

Since then, I have sent many messages to Raphael this way. I still pick up my darts whenever possible and bring them back home with me. On a number of occasions, the dart has taken off and left the park, making it impossible for me to find. On those occasions I am grateful that I still write my messages in invisible ink.

This covers some of the different ways in which you can contact Raphael using his element. In the next chapter we'll look at the specific gemstones that relate to Raphael, and see how they can be used to enhance our relationship with him.

Eight

RAPHAEL AND CRYSTALS

P EOPLE have always been aware of the healing and sacred powers of crystals. Crystals are mentioned many times in the Bible. Aaron, the first High Priest of Israel, wore a religious breastplate containing twelve large gemstones, each inscribed with the name of one of the twelve tribes of Israel (Exodus 28:15–30). These stones contained mysterious and miraculous qualities. When St. John the Apostle described a "New Jerusalem," he mentioned that the foundations of the walls "were garnished with all manner of precious stones." (Revelation 21:19)

Crystals have been important in virtually every other religion, also. They are mentioned in the Talmud and the Koran. The Hindu Puranas describe an amazing jewel-bedecked city called Dwaraka, where Lord Krishna was able to receive his visitors. The ancient Egyptians considered gemstones to be an integral part of their spiritual lives.

Crystals placed on your altar or in your sacred space will encourage angelic visitations. The vibrations of different crystals encourage communication with the angelic kingdom, giving us access to insight, knowledge and healing. Three crystals, celestite, angelite and selenite, are considered to be especially useful when contacting the angelic realms. Rutilated quartz is also important, as it appears to contain trapped strands of angel hair. Not surprisingly, rutilated quartz is frequently known as angel's hair.

Raphael is attracted to many crystals. Any crystal or gemstone that is clear, gold, blue, yellow, white or green appeals to him.

The best way to find the right crystal or crystals for you is to browse in a lapidary store, or any other place where crystals and gemstones are sold. You will find that certain stones respond to your touch, while others have no effect on you whatsoever. Hold as many crystals as you can. Some will virtually speak to you, while others may be unresponsive. As you hold each one, ask yourself how you would best use this particular crystal. Take your time doing this. Sometimes you will receive an immediate answer in your mind, while at other times you may get a feeling that you should buy this particular stone, even though you do not yet have any particular use for it in mind.

You may want to visit the store several times before finally making a purchase. Choose stones that communicate with you. You will have more success with these than with crystals that were chosen solely because they looked attractive.

Once you have bought a crystal, you will need to cleanse it before using it. This removes any negative energies that it may have picked up before coming into your possession. The easiest way to do this is to wash it in salt water. If you live close to the ocean, you will be able to use sea water for this. However, ordinary table salt and tap water work just as well. Once you have washed your crystal, leave it outside to dry naturally in the ultraviolet rays that are present, both night and day.

Another effective way to cleanse your crystal is to bury it in the earth for twenty-four hours. If you live in an apartment, you might want to bury it in the earth surrounding a potted plant.

Raphael's Healing Gems

Green is the color of healing. It brings harmony, balance, contentment, serenity and peace of mind. Can you remember the feelings and sensations you experienced when you walked through the green ray of the rainbow? You are likely to recapture these feelings when working with green gemstones. You should use any green gemstone that appeals to you when calling on Raphael for healing. Here are some of the most commonly used gemstones for this purpose.

Aventurine

Aventurine is a member of the quartz family, and is usually green in color, with bright inclusions of hematite or mica. It has always been considered a useful stone to carry or wear in times of emotional upheaval. It releases stress, anxiety and fear, while enhancing feelings of independence, security and confidence.

Chrysoprase

Chrysoprase is an apple-green, translucent chalcedony. It has been found in the jewelry of Egyptian mummies, showing that its special properties have been recognized for thousands of years. It is the tenth stone mentioned by St. John as being in the foundations of a New Jerusalem (Revelation 22:20). Albertus Magnus claimed that Alexander the Great wore a chrysoprase in his girdle.

Many qualities have been ascribed to chrysoprase. At one time it was believed that if a condemned person placed a chrysoprase in his mouth, he would escape from his execution. This was because the stone would make him invisible. Chrysoprase has always been associated with the eyes. Camillus Leonardus wrote: "Its principle virtue is to cherish the sight. It gives assuity in good works; it banishes covetousness."[1] Its attributes have increased over the years, and today it is believed to provide people who wear it with insight, self-knowledge, and enhanced perception. It encourages the imagination, and allows the wearer to become aware of his or her hidden potential. It is calming and heals the physical and emotional bodies. It can also release people from their addictions.

Chrysoprase was introduced to Europe during the Crusades, and many people thought it was the Holy Grail. Some of the most notable examples of chrysoprase dating from this time can be seen in the Treasury of the Three Magi, in the Dome at Cologne, in West Germany.

Emerald

Emerald is a bright green form of beryl. It is the birthstone of May, because the bright green color symbolizes spring and the rebirth that this season provides. Records survive showing that emeralds were sold in the markets of Babylon six thousand years ago.[2] Cleopatra wore emeralds that came from her own mine in Upper Egypt. The ancient Egyptians believed that this stone increased love and encouraged fertility. Aristotle wrote that emeralds increase the owner's sense of importance in business, ensure success in trials and litigations, and also soothe the eyes. Damigeron, a Roman magician, wrote in the second century B.C.E.: "It influences every kind of business, and if you remain chaste while you wear it, it adds substance to both the body and the speech."[3]

Traditionally, emeralds were believed to enhance the mentality, improve the memory, and purify the thoughts. Emeralds are also considered to act as protective amulets, and deflect negative energies back to where they came from. Emeralds are uplifting and also provide insight into the future. Dreaming about emeralds was considered a sure sign of fame and worldly success in the future.

Emeralds have always been associated with love, kindness and honesty. They demand these qualities from anyone who is performing healing with them.

Green Jade

In China, jade is known as "the concentrated essence of love." A butterfly made of jade symbolizes a long and happy marriage. An old legend tells how a young man accidentally entered a rich mandarin's garden while chasing a butterfly.

He expected to be punished, but instead met the daughter of the mandarin, and later married her. Not surprisingly, young men in China frequently give their fiancées a jade butterfly as a gift. Green jade has always been cherished in the East, and the oldest known character for "emperor" in China is a string of jade beads.

Early Spanish explorers in Central and South America took jade back home to Europe with them, and also inadvertently gave us the name "jade." It comes from *piedra de hijada*, which means "stone of the flank." They called it this after discovering that the local people used jade as a cure for kidney ailments. Today it is still used to help cure all afflictions of the lower abdomen, including renal problems. It also attracts abundance.

Green Jasper

Jasper is a translucent stone that is found throughout the world. It is usually red, yellow, brown, green or blue in color. The famous physician Claudius Galen (c. 130–201 C.E.) wrote that "the green jasper benefits the chest, if tied upon it."[4] Andreas, the tenth-century bishop of Caesarea, wrote:

> The jasper, which like the emerald is of a greenish hue, probably signifies St. Peter, chief of the Apostles, as one who so bore Christ's death in his inmost nature that his love for Him was always vigorous and fresh. By his fervent faith he has become our shepherd and leader.[5]

Traditionally, green jasper is believed to promote confidence and self-esteem, increase love and affection, and expand intuitive awareness. It is a grounding stone, and is important for security, survival and well-being.

Raphael's Gems for Creativity

You can use any gemstone that is yellow, orange or gold in color when using Raphael to enhance your creativity, memory, or learning ability.

Amber

Amber is the fossilized, hardened resin from the pine tree, and was created about fifty million years ago. The oldest three-dimensional works of art in Northern Europe were carved from amber, and are about nine thousand years old. There were many theories as to its origin. The Greek politician Nicias (?–413 B.C.E.) thought that it was the essence of the sun's rays that had broken off as the sun set into the sea.

Amber was originally regarded as a healing stone, and was recommended for the plague, impotence, vertigo, heart disease, and for staunching blood. In medieval times, people felt that it could reveal the presence of poison. Any change in color was felt to be a sign of loss of affection. In the sixteenth century, Leonardus claimed that if amber was "laid on the left breast of a wife when she is asleep, it makes her confess all her evil deeds. If we would discover whether a woman has been corrupted, let it be laid in water for three days, and then shewn to her, and if she is guilty, it will immediately force her to make water."[6]

Today amber is considered a symbol of marital fidelity. It enables both men and women to more easily express their feminine side. It is believed to purify the mind, body and spirit, while drawing out and eliminating negativity. It also enhances recall of previous lives, and enhances concentration and memory.

Beryl

In Roman times, beryl was considered the gemstone of young love, promising great things for lovers who wore it. It was also considered excellent for diseases of the eyes. The afflicted eye had to be washed with water that had had a beryl immersed in it.

In the thirteenth century, Arnoldus Saxo wrote that beryl was a useful form of protection in battle. "The wearer was rendered unconquerable and at the same time amiable, while his intellect was quickened and he was cured of laziness."[7]

In the Middle Ages, the beryl was known as an oracle stone. One method involved using the stone, suspended on a length of thread, as a pendulum. Another method involved dropping the crystal into a bowl of water, and interpreting the disturbances made to the water's surface.[8] It was believed to be especially useful for finding lost or hidden objects. Sir Reginald Scot explained how the beryl was used for divination purposes in his classic book, *The Discoverie of Witchcraft*:

> A child, born in wedlock, was to take the crystal in his hands, and the operator, kneeling behind him, was to repeat a prayer to St. Helen, that what he wished would become evident in the stone. The finest stone would manifest an image of the saint in an angelic form, and answer any question asked of her.[9]

Dreaming of beryl is a sign that you will rise rapidly in your chosen career, and will be respected and honored by others. Beryl brings insight, truth, candor, and a desire to learn.

Carnelian

Carnelian is mentioned in the Egyptian *Book of the Dead* as a protective burial amulet. Although the first of the twelve stones in Aaron's breastplate is said to be sardius, it is generally considered to be a carnelian. Muhammad is believed to have worn a silver ring set with a carnelian seal. Muslims still believe that they are close to God when they wear such a seal.

Carnelians were believed to provide courage, and to enable people to speak with a strong, clear voice. Carnelians are still used today to lessen anxiety and fear, and to promote confidence and self-esteem. It stabilizes the emotions, increases love between family members, and encourages clear thinking. It allows you to focus on the present moment, rather than living in the past or future.

Citrine

The name citrine comes from citron, the French word for lemon. It is called the "wealth stone" as it brings abundance and prosperity to whomever owns it.

Citrine is a warming, comforting and stimulating stone. Consequently, it eliminates negativity, and promotes physical well-being. It has two associations with Raphael. It "protected the wearer from the dangers in travelling."[10] It also provides encouragement and stimulation to anyone who is studying.

Yellow Sapphire

Sapphire is available in a variety of colors, ranging from colorless to black. Since ancient Egyptian times, it has been used to remove foreign objects from the eye, and to help treat diseases of the eye.

It is believed to have a close connection with the spiritual world. The medieval writer Bartolomaeus Anglicus wrote: "Also wytches love well this stone, for they wene that they may werke certen wonders by vertue of this stone."[11]

Raphael's Traditional Gemstones

Raphael is usually associated with clear quartz and diamond.

Quartz

Quartz is an extremely abundant crystal that is found throughout the world. It has always been associated with visions and dreams. Twenty-five hundred years ago, the Greek priest Onomacritis observed: "Who so goes into the temple with this (quartz) in his hand may be quite sure of having his prayer granted, as the gods cannot withstand its power."[12] The ancient Greeks thought that quartz was petrified ice, and this belief persisted until at least the eleventh century. Quartz has always been associated with healing, and has been used to stop bleeding and to control dysentery. It also provides protection from dangerous animals, drowning, fires, and even theft. The sixteenth-century Italian physician Camillus Leonardus wrote: "Crystal (quartz) hung about those who are asleep, keeps off bad dreams;

dissolves spells; being held in the mouth, it assuages thirst; and when bruised with honey, fills the breast with milk."

Today, quartz is used for purification purposes, and to enhance and amplify psychic energy. It can also be programmed with healing thoughts, so that this energy can be imparted to others.

Diamond

Strangely, diamonds were not appreciated until the fourth century B.C.E., when Indian engravers finally became aware of their special qualities. There are a number of biblical references to diamonds that predate this, but that is because the name "diamond" comes from the Greek word adamas, which means "extreme hardness." Consequently, any hard gemstone was called diamond.

Because of its extreme hardness, the diamond has always been considered invincible, and consequently has the power to cure any disease. Saint Hildegarde (1098–1179) claimed that if a diamond was held in one hand, while the other hand made the sign of the cross over it, the curative powers of the diamond would multiply. Marco Polo claimed that the hardness of the diamond ensured that it averted bad luck and all dangers. However, it was widely believed that the talismanic qualities were lost if the diamond was bought. It had to be received as a gift to be effective as a talisman.

How to Dedicate Your Crystal to Raphael

You can dedicate your crystal to Raphael in a variety of ways. The simplest method is to hold it in the palm of your left hand, which is resting on your right palm, and talk to it. Tell the crystal that you want to use it to establish a permanent close connection with Raphael, and that you plan to fill the crystal with positive energy to make that a reality. Tell the crystal everything that occurs to you, and then wait for a response. You may feel a sensation in your left palm as the crystal responds. You may hear a small voice telling you that everything is under control. You may simply experience a sense of knowing, or an overwhelming sensation of love.

A more involved method is to again hold the crystal in your left hand while you sit down comfortably and relax your body. Close your eyes and visualize the crystal in your imagination. Imagine it growing larger and larger until you feel you could walk inside it. Picture yourself, entirely surrounded by your huge crystal. Enjoy the feelings of security and comfort you experience while inside your crystal. Talk to the crystal, and sense your voice echoing inside the large chamber, as you tell it that you intend to devote it to Raphael. Wait for the crystal to respond. It will be delighted to serve this role for you, and you will receive a positive reaction. Talk to the crystal for as long as you wish, then step outside of the crystal and allow it to shrink back to its normal size.

Once you have dedicated your crystal, you can use it to make regular contact with Raphael. You should hold it when communicating with Raphael. Hold it whenever you pray or say affirmations. If you write letters to Raphael, you can place them under the crystal overnight, confident that he will receive them. It is a good idea to carry or wear the crystal, so that any time you feel the need for Raphael's comfort or support, all you need do is touch your crystal.

Dowsing with a Crystal

Most people associate dowsing with water divining, but this is only part of what dowsing can do. You can dowse for items, such as gold, oil, lost objects, or stolen property. You can also use it for other purposes, such as testing food for freshness, or for determining what movie to see on Saturday night. You can also dowse to obtain advice and help from the angelic realms.

First of all, you will need a crystal pendulum. You can buy these from occult and New Age stores, as well as many gift shops. A pendulum is a small weight attached to a thread or chain. Once you have found a pendulum that appeals to you, hold it by the thread between the thumb and first finger of your dominant hand. You will find it helpful to rest the elbow of that arm on a table and allow the pendulum to swing to and fro an inch or so above the table's surface.

Stop the movements of the pendulum with your free hand, and then ask the pendulum which movement indicates "yes." There are four possibilities. The pendulum will move from side to side, or toward and away from you, or in a circular motion, clockwise or counterclockwise. Once you have determined "yes," ask for a "no" response. Follow this by asking for "I don't know" and "I don't want to answer" responses.

Practice by asking the pendulum questions to which you already know the answers. You might start by asking if your name is whatever it happens to be. The pendulum should respond with a "yes." Then ask if you are, say, thirty years old. If this is your current age, the pendulum should say "yes." Obviously, if you are not, it should give a negative response.

Once you have tested the pendulum and are receiving correct answers all the time, ask it some questions to which you do not know the answers, but which you can confirm. You might, for example, ask the pendulum if your partner is currently at the supermarket. Note the response that the pendulum gives you, and then confirm the correctness of the reply with your partner when he or she arrives home. If your partner has a cell phone, you can immediately verify what the pendulum tells you. You might ask about several locations, until the pendulum confirms that your partner is at a certain place, and then call them to check.

Once the pendulum has proved itself to you, you can start using it to contact Raphael. Start by sitting in your sacred space and spending a few minutes in quiet meditation, relaxing your mind and body. When you feel ready, pick up the pendulum and tell it that you want to use it to communicate with Raphael. Is the pendulum happy to be used in this way? The pendulum should give a positive response. Ask Raphael to join you. If you have done many of the earlier exercises you will probably know when Raphael has arrived, but the pendulum will alert you anyway, by giving a positive response.

You can now ask Raphael any questions that can be answered by the four possible responses. You can ask Raphael anything at all. Talk about your hopes and dreams, and ask Raphael questions about how you can achieve them. When you have finished, thank Raphael for all his help, and then say "good-bye." The pendulum will give a positive response. Think about the communication you have just had with Raphael for a minute or two before getting up.

You may wonder why anyone would dowse for answers from Raphael when you can simply ask him the questions using one of the methods we have already covered. Everyone is different, and some people receive better results by dowsing for the answers than they do from any of the other methods.

It is a good idea to experiment with a variety of methods. You may find that one method works well at one time, while another method appeals to you more on another occasion. When I was training to become a hypnotherapist, we were taught many different methods to hypnotize people. This was to prevent us from becoming "one trick ponies," able to hypnotize people with one method only. After all, the clients we were going to be dealing with were all different, and a method that worked well for one client might not be nearly as successful on another occasion, or with another client. The same thing applies with angelic contact. You are bound to find one or two methods that you enjoy more than the others, but it is useful to be able to utilize other methods from time to time, as well.

Crystals have many purposes. You can use them as amulets to keep Raphael close to you at all times. With Raphael's help, you can also use them to heal yourself and others. Crystals play an important role in chakra healing, also. Chakras are spinning wheels of energy inside your aura. You will discover Raphael's role in keeping your chakras in good shape in the next chapter.

Nine

RAPHAEL
AND THE CHAKRAS

YOU are surrounded by an invisible ovoid bubble known as your aura. Your aura is an extension of your physical body, and it expands and contracts depending on a variety of circumstances, such as your current degree of energy, enthusiasm and health. Although most people cannot see it, your aura glows with all the colors of the rainbow. There are many books available that can teach you the art of seeing and reading auras.[1]

Inside the aura are seven spiritual centers, full of energy, called chakras. Five of these are aligned along the spinal column, and the other two are located in the head. The word chakra comes from the Sanskrit and means "wheel." The chakras received this name as they are usually seen as whirling orbs of energy. Each chakra is associated with a specific color. In one sense they can be seen as a spiritual ladder that leads to enlightenment. Ideally, each chakra is well-balanced and working efficiently. In reality, though, emotional problems and stress frequently cause problems in the chakras that then become reflected in the physical body.

Root Chakra

Color: Red
Archangel: Sandalphon
Crystals: Bloodstone, red garnet, jasper, ruby

The root, or base, chakra is situated at the base of the spine and is concerned with grounding, survival, self-preservation, vitality and strength. When this chakra is well-balanced the person feels grounded and in control of every aspect of his or her life. Blockages in this chakra make the person aggressive and stubborn.

Sacral Chakra

Color: Orange
Archangel: Chamuel
Crystals: Amber, carnelian, moonstone, orange calcite, topaz

The sacral chakra is situated between the navel and the genitals. It is concerned with creativity, security and the person's sex life. When it is well-balanced the person feels positive, optimistic and in tune with his or her feelings. This person will also be concerned with the happiness and well-being of others. Blockages in this chakra can cause frigidity and a sense of being totally alone.

Solar Chakra

Color: Yellow

Archangel: Uriel

Crystals: Citrine, tiger's eye, yellow jasper

The solar chakra is situated one inch above the navel. This chakra is concerned with logic, the intellect, and goals. When this chakra is well-balanced the person will be outgoing, friendly, relaxed and generous. Blockages in this chakra can lead to mental problems.

Heart Chakra

Color: Green

Archangel: Raphael

Crystals: Aventurine, emerald, jade, kunzite

The heart chakra is situated in the center of the chest, in the area of the heart. It is concerned with compassion, acceptance, relationships and love. This includes both physical love and an unconditional love for all humanity. When this chakra is well-balanced, the person is compassionate, kind, and in touch with his or her feelings. Not surprisingly, blockages in this chakra make it hard for the person to express his or her feelings.

Throat Chakra

Color: Blue

Archangel: Michael

Crystals: Aquamarine, chrysocolla, lapis lazuli, turquoise

The throat chakra is situated in the throat, and is concerned with self-expression, creativity, the truth, and communication, especially verbal communication. When this chakra is well-balanced the person is contented, creative, inspirational and spiritual. Blockages in this chakra cause the person to become inflexible and controlling.

Brow Chakra

Color: Indigo
Archangel: Gabriel
Crystals: Amethyst, blue calcite, lapis lazuli, turquoise

This chakra is situated between the eyebrows, and is concerned with inner vision, insight, wisdom, intuition and self-respect. When this chakra is well-balanced the person is unattached to possessions, has no fear of death, and is interested in developing clairvoyantly and spiritually. Blockages in this chakra cause the person to drift aimlessly through life.

Crown Chakra

Color: Violet
Archangel: Zadkiel
Crystals: Amethyst, charoite, clear quartz, selenite

The crown chakra is situated immediately above the crown of the head. It is concerned with illumination, understanding and spirituality. It opens us up to divine energy. All the finer human qualities, such as compassion, devotion, sacrifice and kindness, are represented here. Blockages in this chakra cause feelings of isolation and loss of faith.

Balancing Your Chakras

You can use your pendulum to assess the state of your chakras. Ask your pendulum if your root chakra is balanced. Then ask about each of the other chakras in turn. If they are all in a state of balance, you will receive seven positive messages from your pendulum, and can stop at this point. However, if one or more of the chakras are out of balance, you will need to harmonize them. You can do this in a variety of ways.

One effective method is to close your eyes, and breathe in quantities of the color that relates to the unbalanced chakra. Visualize the color entering your body and swirling around in the area of the chakra. After visualizing this for a minute or two, test the chakra again with your pendulum. Repeat as many times as are necessary, until your pendulum gives you a positive response.

Another method is to lie down, and ask Raphael to join you. Place a crystal that relates to the specific chakra over the unbalanced chakra and leave it there for several minutes while discussing anything you wish with Raphael. Once you have done this, ask Raphael to bless the crystal for you. Keep the crystal with you for the rest of the day, and handle it as much as possible.

You can energize and harmonize all of the chakras by going through the rainbow meditation in chapter 6. Focus on each chakra in turn as you bathe yourself in the different colors.

After you have done this, it can be a good idea to walk back through the rainbow again, gently closing each chakra in turn. The reason for this is that you make yourself vulnerable to outside interference when all your chakras are left stimulated and open. You are not shutting them down by closing them in this way. All you are doing is dampening them so that they are harmonized, balanced and at ease. You might choose to walk back through the rainbow and see yourself turning off some of the lights, so that the colors are not quite as bright or intense. You might prefer to imagine that you are partly closing doors or pulling down blinds. It makes no difference what you choose to do, just as long as you feel that you are quieting each chakra.

Occasionally, you might find yourself in a situation when you need to quickly close your chakras. You might choose to do this if you find yourself in an extremely stressful or negative situation. In an emergency of this sort, quickly go through the colors of the rainbow, starting with violet, and say to yourself "close" as you visualize the color. By doing this you can close your chakras in a matter of seconds. Remember though, to energize them again as soon as possible afterward, by walking leisurely through the rainbow.

Your Heart Chakra

As Raphael is the archangel of healing, he will be happy to work with you on balancing any or all of your chakras. However, the chakra he is specifically associated with is the heart chakra.

You have probably experienced sensations of overwhelming love in your heart chakra at times of great emotion. This is a warm, overwhelming, expanding feeling that fills your upper chest with love. At these times your heart chakra opens wide. I am sure you can remember many moments when this occurred. I remember experiencing it when I watched my younger son walk on stage during a school play when he was seven years old. Seeing my granddaughter for the first time when she was just a few minutes old is another occasion when this occurred. These are the first thoughts that immediately come to mind when I think about the spontaneous responses of my heart chakra.

The heart chakra is extremely vulnerable to the positive and negative aspects of love. Unfortunately, many people close their heart chakras when they are let down or badly hurt in a relationship. They tell themselves that they will never let anyone do that to them again, and then ensure it does not happen by closing down the chakra. The same thing occurs when someone goes through a tragedy, but does not allow him- or herself sufficient time to go through the grieving process. In effect, the person becomes numb and empty inside.

Emotional problems relating to the heart chakra are more common in women than men. This can be explained through the chakras. The male sex organs are situated in the root chakra, and this energy can easily be applied to the third chakra, which is the seat of personal power. The female sex organs are situated in the sacral chakra, and this energy is naturally applied to the heart chakra, the seat of universal love.

The heart chakra is closely associated with the crown chakra. The crown chakra is concerned with universal consciousness and divine love, while the heart chakra is the center for love, compassion, affection, joy, concern and other higher human emotions. When you work on developing the qualities of your heart chakra, you are also developing the crown chakra qualities of divine love and enlightenment.

This is beneficial for a number of reasons. In most people the lower three chakras are reasonably well-developed. They relate to survival, the sex urge, and willpower. The mental chakras (throat and brow) are also active in many people, as great emphasis is placed on intellectual development nowadays. Unfortunately, this means that the heart and crown chakras tend to be neglected. A good example of this is someone who is well-educated, but is also emotionally immature.

Some years ago I worked with a man who was extremely well-qualified in his profession, but had a string of disastrous relationships behind him. He came to me for help because he had unintentionally reacted physically during an argument with his girlfriend, and was concerned that if it happened again, he might cause serious damage. In his case, the solar chakra was overdeveloped at the expense of his heart chakra.

Obviously, anyone who is aware that his or her heart chakra is underdeveloped should ask Raphael for help. Raphael wants you to be a whole person in every way. This is impossible when your heart chakra is blocked.

Assessing Your Heart Chakra

Sit down comfortably and close your eyes. Focus on your breathing for a minute or two, and then bring your attention to the area of your heart. Become aware of your heart chakra, and determine how open it is. The heart chakra is an extremely active one, and you may find that it is wide open. If this is the case, you might want to slow it down slightly. Focus on slowing it down, and stop when it reaches what feels like the right rate for you. Alternatively, your heart chakra might be closed, in which case you need to gently open it until it feels comfortable for you.

Now allow yourself to enter into the chakra itself. Take your time doing this. If it seems too emotional or heavy, draw back for a while, and call on Raphael to help you. Wait until he arrives and then try again. Once inside the chakra, think about the love in your life, and see what responses your heart chakra gives to you. Repeat the word "love" several times, and notice what feelings this word creates inside the chakra.

Allow your heart chakra to fill up with green energy, and sense the feelings of total, perfect, unconditional love. Allow these feelings to gradually reach out into every part of your body. Take note of any ideas or insights that occur to you while this is going on.

Now it is time to leave the heart chakra. Focus on the green color inside the chakra, and allow it to become slightly duller. This is to partially close down your heart chakra after the stimulation this exercise will have created. If Raphael has helped you with this exercise, thank him at this point, as the assessment is now complete.

Become aware of your root chakra, and imagine it connected to the ground by an invisible tube of energy. Feel yourself grounded to the earth through this tube. When you feel ready, open your eyes.

Re-Activating Your Heart Chakra

Jesus said: "A new commandment I give unto you, That ye love one another; as I have loved you, that ye also love one another." (John 13:34) Many people lead sad, lonely, loveless lives because their heart chakra is blocked. Fortunately, the heart chakra can be re-activated again, no matter how long it has been closed down. However, the person must realize that he or she has a problem, and also have a sincere desire to change. It is a ten-step process.

1. Start by taking some brisk exercise. This is not only good for your physical body, but it also energizes your entire aura. It makes no difference what exercise you do, but you should be slightly breathless at the end of it. This will increase your heart rate temporarily.

2. Make sure that you will not be disturbed for about thirty minutes. Lie down and make yourself comfortable. Take several deep breaths and relax as much as possible.

3. Walk through the rainbow, focusing on each chakra in turn as you go through the colors.

4. Once you emerge on the far side of the rainbow, visualize yourself in the most beautiful and peaceful setting you can imagine. Spend as long as you wish enjoying the pleasant sights, sounds and smells of this magical place.

5. When you feel ready, look up at the beautiful, clear blue sky, and in your mind's eye, visualize

Raphael looking down at you with a pleasant, but concerned, smile on his face. He knows why you are performing this particular meditation, and he is prepared and willing to help. As you gaze up at him, you notice that he is holding a small green ball. He lightly tosses it from hand to hand as he looks back at you. As you watch, he tosses the ball into the air, and now this beautiful emerald-green ball is coming down toward you.

6. The ball slowly and gently heads directly to you. You know instinctively that you do not need to catch it, and you watch as the ball hovers close to your heart, and then disappears inside your body.

7. You can feel the warmth of the green ball as it gently massages and stimulates your heart chakra. You feel a quickness in your heart, and an overwhelming sensation of love and peace comes over you.

8. Lie in this beautiful, peaceful place for as long as you wish, enjoying the joyful effects of the green energy as it transforms and revitalizes your heart chakra, and then sends love throughout your entire body. You look up at Raphael and notice that he is still smiling, but the concern has vanished from his face. He laughs and waves to you. You laugh and wave back, and watch as he slowly fades from sight.

9. Get up, stretch, and walk back through the rainbow, turning off a light or two in each color as you pass through.

10. Become aware of yourself, lying in your comfortable space. Think about the experience and sense the change in the area of your heart. Open your eyes, stretch, and get up. Allow yourself a few minutes to gather your thoughts and to think about what has happened before continuing with your day.

Some people find this meditation highly emotional. It is important to let the emotion out. It may have been blocked for a long time, and restoring your heart chakra can be like opening up a dam that has held back a huge amount of pain and emotion. Consequently, you can cry, shout, or punch a pillow until you feel that all the pent-up emotion has been released. Once you have done this, enjoy a cleansing shower or bath before returning to your day.

How to Express Universal Love All the Time

The state of your heart chakra affects every aspect of your attitude toward love. When your heart chakra is balanced, you will be able to give and receive love readily. People who meet you for the first time will be subliminally aware that you are a caring, loving, concerned person who has everybody's well-being at heart. Whether you are aware of it or not, when your heart chakra is well-balanced, you express universal love. When you are in this state, you will naturally attract other people to you. You will also be poised, confident, calm, and sure of yourself. You will love yourself and have good self-esteem. You will love others and you will love life. Small things will not bother or upset you. You will be able to focus on what is important, and ignore or dismiss the petty small aspects of life that hold back other people. Another beneficial side effect is that a well-balanced heart chakra makes you appear more attractive to others.

Imagine what the world would be like if everyone had a healthy, well-balanced heart chakra. There would finally be peace and harmony in the world. The French Jesuit priest and philosopher, Teilhard de Chardin (1881–1955), may have been thinking along these lines when he wrote:

> Someday, after we have mastered
> the winds, the waves, the tide
> and gravity, we shall harness for God
> the energies of love.
> Then, for the second time in the history
> Of the world, man will have discovered fire.[2]

Teilhard de Chardin believed that love was the mysterious force that connects all the elements of the world.

With the help of Raphael, you can have a well-balanced heart chakra all the time. In one of your meditations with Raphael, ask him to help you achieve this goal, so that you can make a difference in the world. He will be happy to help you achieve this, and may give you suggestions as to how you can reach it. Perform the rainbow meditation frequently and pause for a while under the green rays each time, to allow your body to absorb as much beneficial, healing energy as possible.

As a child I attended a church school. At least once every semester, the head prefect would stand up in chapel and read to us the famous words of St. Paul to the Corinthians that starts: "If I speak in the tongues of men and of angels, but have not love, I am a noisy gong or a clanging cymbal." (1 Corinthians 13:1) The reading always finished with: "So faith, hope, love abide, these three; but the greatest of these is love." (1 Corinthians 13:13)[3]

Giving and Receiving Love with Your Heart Chakra

This is a modern version of an ancient ritual devised by Atiśa (982–1054), an Indian Buddhist reformer, writer and teacher. Place two straight-backed chairs about a yard apart, facing each other. Sit in one of them and close your eyes. Allow your arms to hang loosely at your sides.

Imagine that Raphael is sitting in the other chair, facing you. Inhale deeply, absorbing Raphael's energy as you do so. Visualize Raphael's love circling in the area of your heart chakra. Hold your breath for a few moments and then exhale. This time visualize yourself sending love back to Raphael.

Do this once, and then sit quietly for at least sixty seconds. Become aware of what is going on inside your body, and take note of any thoughts that occur to you.

Repeat the exercise, breathing in deeply and absorbing as much of Raphael's energy as you can. Hold the breath and exhale slowly, sending your love back to Raphael.

Again sit quietly for at least sixty seconds, and notice what is going on in your mind and body. You can finish the ritual at this point, if you wish. However, there are two additional stages that you will find helpful in everyday life. All three stages can be done separately, but I usually practice all three together.

In your imagination, become aware that Raphael has stood up and is now standing on your right-hand side. Visualize someone who is important to you taking his place on the chair. This might be your partner, a relative, a friend, someone you work with, and even someone whom you actually dislike.

Picture that person as clearly as possible in your mind. Take a deep breath in, drawing in that person's energy as you do so. Allow it to swirl in the area of your heart. Hold the breath for a few seconds, and then exhale, sending love back to that person.

Sit quietly for at least sixty seconds, and become aware of your thoughts and what is going on inside your body. Repeat the exercise again, and see what occurs to you. (This exercise is an extremely helpful one in developing closer relationships with everyone in your life. Experiment with people whom you love, as well as those you dislike, and feel the different energies inside your heart chakra.)

The third and final stage is to send universal love out to the world. Imagine that the chair facing you has disappeared, and that you are on top of a mountain looking out across the whole world. Notice how beautiful it appears. Raphael is still standing beside you, and may rest a hand upon your shoulder. Inhale deeply, absorbing energy from the earth itself. Hold it, and then send universal love back in return. Pause for sixty seconds, and then repeat. (If you wish, you can repeat this stage, sending out love to all living things.)

When you have finished, thank Raphael for his help and support, open your eyes, and stretch or move around for a few minutes before doing anything else.

Praying with Your Heart Chakra

In the Sermon on the Mount, Jesus exhorts the people to "seek ye first the kingdom of God . . . and all things shall be added unto you." (Matthew 6:33) A logical question might be: "Where is the kingdom of God?" If you pause and think about this question, you will probably come to the conclusion that it is actually inside your own heart. The heart is considered the home of God in many societies. People pledge oaths by placing a hand upon the heart, because it symbolizes truth, honesty and love. In China the heart is called "the Lord and Master of the House."[4]

Your prayers will become more effective once you allow them to come from your heart chakra. Before starting to pray, spend a few minutes sending green energy to your heart chakra, and visualize it expanding and growing as a result. Once you have done that, say your prayers, but imagine them being sent to the universal life force from your heart chakra. You are likely to find this a strange and possibly uncomfortable feeling at first. However, once you become used to it, you will learn that it is a natural and extremely effective way of praying.

You can also use your heart chakra to enhance your creativity. You will learn how to do this in the next chapter.

Ten

RAPHAEL
AND CREATIVITY

CREATIVITY is the ability to bring something new into existence. Each time you come up with the solution to a problem, or bring something about, you are using your natural creativity. When you sing or play a musical instrument, you are creating music. When you tell someone about a movie you have seen, you are creating pictures in his or her mind. You create something whenever you work in the garden, take a photograph, or cook a meal. Every time you think a thought you are being creative. In fact, you are creating your own life on a daily basis. Your power to create is unlimited.

Although this is a natural faculty that we all possess, many people tell me they are not creative. However, this is not the case, as everyone has between fifty and sixty thousand thoughts a day. This means that everyone is highly creative.

All human beings possess an imagination, and by using it creatively, can create anything they wish in their minds. This mental image is the first stage of creation. Nothing would ever happen unless someone thought of it first. Every man-made object that you can name was the result of someone's creativity, and was usually the solution to a problem or difficulty. Inventors are highly creative people who think about problems and come up with solutions.

Of course, some people are naturally more creative than others, and even highly creative people differ enormously. Two of my friends are writers. One is a journalist who reports facts, and the other writes romance novels. This means that she uses her imagination to come up with her characters and plots. Both earn their living from the words they produce. Are these two people equally creative, or is the fiction writer more creative because she invents her material? It is impossible to answer this question. However, I feel that they are equally creative, but utilize it in different ways.

Intelligence appears to have little bearing on how creative someone will be. Someone with a high IQ, but little imagination, may be highly analytical and brilliant in his or her field, but is unlikely to demonstrate outstanding creativity. Conversely, someone with a lower IQ, but an inquiring mind that questions everything, may well be highly creative. Highly creative people are often unconventional, and this gives them a slightly different slant on life, which encourages creativity.

However, creativity is something that can be developed. After all, if we think up to sixty thousand thoughts a day, we can certainly manage to produce a few creative ideas along the way.

More importantly, our whole purpose in life is to create. Once you know your purpose in life, it will be naturally expressed by your innate creative nature. A sculptor, for example, has to sculpt. It is his purpose in life. If he suddenly won a million dollars, he would not stop working, but would continue to create. A friend of mine has become a multi-millionaire from his writing. He writes action-packed thrillers that sell around the world. Although he has always found writing an enormous struggle, he is continuing to write his books because that is his purpose in life. He could retire tomorrow, but that would bring him no joy or satisfaction, because all the meaning and purpose to his life would disappear.

Of course, it all becomes much easier once you have found your purpose. Once you find what you love, you can then pursue it with a passion. If you have not yet discovered your purpose, ask Raphael to help you find it.

Take your time doing this. You may have a sudden burst of inspiration in which your life's purpose is revealed to you, but it is more likely to come as a gradual awareness that a certain activity is what you are here to do. Start by evaluating all the things you enjoy doing. Think about your natural talents. Daydream about various things you would like to do if time and money were no object. Tell Raphael that you need to find your purpose, as you want to make a difference, and create a magnificent life for yourself. Be patient, and carefully evaluate any ideas that come to you.

Raphael is vitally interested in creativity, and will be happy to help you develop the creative side of your nature further. If you have a problem and have been unable to think of a solution, you should ask Raphael for his advice. His response will give you suggestions about the best way to handle the situation.

Creativity is one of the greatest joys of life. The process of creating something is what is important. Consequently, you need not be concerned that what you create is not good enough. It does not have to be perfect. A beginning artist who is still learning how to paint may derive more enjoyment from his or her creativity than a professional artist does. Creativity is something that should provide enormous pleasure and satisfaction.

Creativity Exercises

There are many exercises that are designed to enhance creativity. One method I find helpful is to find three nouns at random in a dictionary. I do this by opening up the dictionary at any page and choosing the first noun I find. I do this twice more to get the other nouns. I then write a paragraph or two that incorporates all three nouns. I sometimes make it harder for myself by insisting that the paragraph starts with one of the words I chose.

You can also do this exercise by deliberately choosing three words that relate to a specific situation. This can be an effective way to solve a problem. If, for example, you were having problems with your boss at work, you might use the words: boss, disagreements, and stress. By using those three words in a paragraph or two, you might find a creative solution to the problem.

A writer friend of mine was suffering from writer's block. I suggested he do this exercise using words that related to the novel he was writing. To his amazement, once he had written the paragraph, he was able to keep on writing his story. This exercise energized his latent creativity, and totally eliminated his writer's block.

Mandalas

Mandalas are an Eastern aid to meditation. As they depict your world at the time you construct it, they are sometimes used as therapeutic tools. All you need is some paper and colored pencils or pens.

Start by drawing a shape that is pleasing to you. Most mandalas are circular, but you can use any shape that appeals to you. Carl Jung studied mandalas for many years and felt that a circle symbolized the cosmos as a whole, while a square symbolized a universe conceived by man. Incidentally, he believed that mandalas represented the divinity incarnate in man.[1]

Choose one of the colored pens and draw something inside the shape, or possibly shade in part of it. Change colors as frequently as you wish, and keep on doing this until you feel ready to stop.

Obviously, this is a creative exercise as you are constructing a picture. However, when you look at your mandala later, you are also likely to receive insights into what is going on in your life. It can be a useful practice to draw a mandala every day for a period of weeks or months, and then go back over them. They will reveal what was going on in your inner life during that time.

You can take this a step further by inviting Raphael to join you, and then creating a mandala in his presence. Compare this with mandalas that you created on your own, and see what difference Raphael's presence made.

You can also construct mandalas while thinking about something that is going on in your life. If you are trying to find your purpose in life, for instance, think about this while drawing a mandala. Your subconscious mind may provide you with useful information that you do not discover until you examine the mandala later.

An acquaintance of mine did this while going through some relationship difficulties. He was alarmed at the anger he saw in his mandalas, but studying them also gave him the knowledge he needed to resolve the situation.

Exploring the Unknown

A highly effective way of developing your creativity is to deliberately do something that you have not considered before. One of my students is now a gourmet cook. He discovered this talent only when I challenged everyone in the class to attempt something new. Another student from the same class discovered quilting. Neither would have become aware of these talents if they had not chosen to do something different.

I kept bees for several years. It was an absorbing interest that gave me enormous pleasure and satisfaction. I deliberately took up this avocation because it was completely different from anything I had tried before. Paper making is another hobby I pursued for some time as a result of this particular exercise.

It makes no difference what the new activity is. In many ways, the more unusual it is, the better. You will learn a great deal of information about something new and different. This increases your knowledge of the world. You may find you have a talent at whatever it happens to be. You may make new friends as a result. You will also expand your natural creativity.

You can involve Raphael in this exercise, also. While communicating with him, ask him to help you brainstorm some activities that you could do. Tell him that you want ideas that are stimulating and will help you develop more creativity. Do not evaluate any of the ideas as they come into your mind. There is plenty of time for that later.

After the session is over, write down all of the suggestions and then think about each one in turn. Something that you might have discarded at first glance may intrigue you once you think about it later. Choose four or five possibilities, and then call on Raphael again to help you choose the right one to start with. You want an activity that is challenging, stimulating, and possibly even slightly frightening. Once you have decided on a single activity, learn as much as you can about it, and then practice it.

Obviously, many activities that you start as a result of this exercise will not hold your interest for long. That is not important. What is important is that you have moved out of your comfort zone and done something different.

Chakra Creativity Exercise

This exercise is a useful one which involves the chakras in receiving and testing creative ideas. You can use it to evaluate an idea you already have, or to come up with new ideas.

Sit or lie down comfortably, and relax in your usual manner. Ask Raphael to join you. When he arrives tell him what you intend doing, and the outcome you desire. Walk through the rainbow with Raphael, allowing the energy from each color to revitalize your chakras.

After emerging from the violet ray, picture yourself in the most beautiful scene you can imagine. Walk through the landscape with Raphael, and find a suitable place where you can sit and brainstorm.

When you are comfortable, tell Raphael about your idea, if you already have something in mind. If you are still looking for inspiration, tell him the sort of thing you are looking for. Discuss this for as long as you wish. Do not hesitate to tell him about your ideas, and listen carefully to Raphael's suggestions.

Once you have decided on a specific idea and it is clear in your mind, ask your heart chakra how it feels about it. You may feel a positive, expansive glow in your chest, telling you that your heart chakra likes the idea. You may experience a tightening, constricting feeling that tells you your heart chakra does not like the idea. You may feel nothing at all, which indicates a neutral response from your heart chakra.

If you received a positive response from your heart chakra, ask your sacral chakra what it thinks about the idea. Your second chakra is involved with creativity, and will respond in the same sort of way as your heart chakra.

If your sacral chakra also gave you a positive reaction, ask your throat chakra about the idea. This chakra is involved with self-expression and communication. If you are going to get your idea off the ground, you will need the support of this chakra.

After this, discuss the idea with Raphael again. Tell him how each chakra felt as it evaluated the idea. See if he has any reservations, or suggestions. If your basic idea is altered as a result of this conversation, ask the chakras for their input again.

Once you are happy with the idea, walk leisurely back through the rainbow with Raphael. Thank him for his help. Become aware of where you are sitting or lying. When you feel ready, open your eyes, stretch, and start implementing the idea.

Creating a Life

You are a perfect human being. Naturally, there are probably aspects of yourself that you would like to change, but deep down you are whole and perfect. Naturally, you'll have problems and difficulties from time to time as you progress through life. Everyone goes through different experiences to learn the lessons that need to be mastered in this lifetime.

Some of these will be of a karmic nature. Karma is the law of cause and effect. A good deed done today will result in something pleasant happening to you in the future. That is good karma. However, something done with an evil intent also has to be paid back in the future. That is negative karma. Raphael cannot remove these karmic debts as they are lessons that need to be learned so that your soul can progress. However, Raphael is always willing to help you handle your karma, and to provide you with wholeness and unity.

Many of the problems that occur with wholeness and unity stem from a lack of self-acceptance. Life is more enjoyable when you accept yourself as you are. Like everyone else, you are a complex mixture of positive and negative traits, and these may have made you feel bad or unworthy.

Have you ever held on to a grievance or grudge for a long time? I certainly have. Feelings of this sort cause tension and stress in the body. Conflicts of any sort have an emotional response on the body, which may ultimately lead to physical problems. Difficult though it may be, it is much healthier to simply let the grievance go.

The Eastern method of "going with the flow," of accepting what has happened, and refusing to resist or fight the inevitable leads to unity and wholeness. It does not mean that you should allow others to trample all over you, or that you should meekly accept everything that is put onto you. All it means is bending, rather than resisting. Once you start doing this, every aspect of your life will be smoother, easier and more enjoyable.

Most of the time our problems in life are caused by our egos. Once we manage to let go of this "I" inside us, and flow with the eternal rhythm of life, we can start to harness it and work with it, and create a worthwhile, meaningful life.

Raphael is willing to help you create the best possible life for you. In your regular sessions with him, ask him for advice whenever you need it.

Eleven

CONCLUSION

A S you have learned, Archangel Raphael has many roles, and is willing to help you in many different ways. He wants you to achieve the sort of life you have always dreamed about. With his help, there is no limit to what you can achieve. Once you start working with him you will realize that your destiny comes from the future, rather than the past. What you were is not important, as long as you have learned from the mistakes of the past. What matters is how you live in the present, and what you become in the future. Raphael is willing to be your guide and mentor, and will help you at every stage as you progress in this lifetime.

I have seen the results of Raphael's help in many people's lives, and know he can do the same for you. All you need do is ask. In return, help him as much as you can by looking after the environment.

Read as much as you can about the angelic kingdom. Ask the angels to help you grow in wisdom and understanding. Become acquainted with your guardian angel. There are many books that can help you do this.[1] Communicate with your guardian angel and the archangels as often as you can. You will become a great deal more spiritual as a result of doing this, and these encounters will have a positive effect on every area of your life.

I hope this book has given you plenty of material to think about and work with. Now it is up to you. I wish you great success.

Notes

Introduction

1. Thomas Aquinas, quoted in: Karl Barth, *Church Dogmatics*, 3 volumes (Edinburgh, Scotland: T & T Clark Limited, 1960), Volume 3, 391.

2. Richard Webster, *Spirit Guides and Angel Guardians* (St. Paul, MN: Llewellyn Publications, 1998), XV–XVI.

3. Harvey Humann, *The Many Faces of Angels* (Marina del Rey, CA: DeVorss and Company, 1986), 30.

Chapter One

1. Anna Jameson, *Sacred and Legendary Art*, Volume 1 (Boston and New York: Houghton Mifflin and Company, 1895), 119.

2. Louis Ginzberg, *The Legends of the Jews*, Volume 1 (Philadelphia, PA: The Jewish Publication Society of America, 1954), 385.

3. Asmodeus is described as an "evil spirit" in *The Book of Tobit* (3:8). He is considered one of the most dangerous of all demons, and was also thought to be the demon of lust. He is believed to have made Noah drunk, and to have invented music, dancing and dreams. Today he is in charge of all the gambling establishments in hell. (Gustav Davidson, *A Dictionary of Angels*, 57–58.)

4. Matthew Black, *The Book of Enoch or 1 Enoch* (Leiden, Netherlands: E. J. Brill, 1985), 129.

5. *The Book of the Angel Raziel* was written in medieval times. It is believed to have been written by either Isaac the Blind or Eleazer of Worms.

6. Frederick G. Conybeare, "The Testament of Solomon." Article in *Jewish Quarterly Review 11* (1898), 1–45. For further information on the medical aspects of the pentagram see: Dr. J. Schouten, *The Pentagram as a Medical Symbol* (Nieuwkoop, Netherlands: De Graaf, 1968).

7. *The Testament of Solomon* is included in *The Old Testament Pseudepigrapha*, 2 volumes, edited by James H. Charlesworth (New York, NY: Doubleday and Company, 1983), 1960–87.

8. Anna Jameson, *Sacred and Legendary Art*, Volume 1, 122.

9. For at least one thousand years people have debated the attribution of Raphael to Mercury. In some traditions,

Michael is assigned to Mercury and Raphael looks after
the Sun. In other traditions, the reverse is the case. This
is because there are two main systems of the Kabbalah.
Judaic Kabbalah, dating back to the time of Moses, has
been passed down through the ages in an oral tradition.
In the Bible, Archangel Michael is named as the angel of
Israel (Daniel 12:1). Consequently, in the Judaic system,
Michael is placed in the pre-eminent position of the
Sun, leaving Mercury for Raphael. Alchemical Kabbalah
uses symbolism drawn from the esoteric mysteries of
the Mediterranean. Their pre-eminent angel is
Archangel Raphael, who can be related to the Greek
god Apollo. Apollo, of course, was associated with healing, science and education. Consequently, in their system, Raphael is connected with the Sun, while Michael
looks after Mercury. I have chosen to use the older
Judaic system in this book.

Chapter Two

1. You might consider buying a book of symbols to help
   you interpret your doodles. There are many to choose
   from. One I find particularly useful and accessible is:
   *Dictionary of Symbols: An Illustrated Guide to Tradi-
   tional Images, Icons and Emblems* by Jack Tresidder
   (San Francisco, CA: Chronicle Books, 1998).

Chapter Five

1. Deborah Lippman and Paul Colin, *How to Make
   Amulets, Charms and Talismans: What They Mean
   and How to Use Them* (New York, NY: M. Evans and
   Company, Inc., 1974), 99.

2. J. Schouten, *The Pentagram as a Medical Symbol* (Nieuwkoop, Netherlands, De Graaf, 1968), 15.

3. R. E. Goodenough, *Jewish Symbols in the Greco-Roman Period, Volume 1: The Archaeological Evidence from Palestine,* 13 volumes (New York, NY: Pantheon Books, 1953), Volume 1, 187.

4. R. E. Goodenough, *Jewish Symbols in the Greco-Roman Period, Volume 1: The Archaeological Evidence from Palestine*, 68.

5. Henry Cornelius Agrippa of Nettesheim, *Three Books of Occult Philosophy,* edited and annotated by Donald Tyson (St. Paul, MN: Llewellyn Publications, 1993), 347.

6. Henry Cornelius Agrippa of Nettesheim, *Three Books of Occult Philosophy*, 564.

7. Diodorus, quoted in *Numbers: Their Occult Power and Mystic Virtues* by W. Wynn Westcott (London, UK: The Theosophical Publishing House Limited, 1890), 62.

8. R. Brasch, *The Supernatural and You!* (Stanmore, Australia: Cassell Australia Limited, 1976), 202.

9. Riane Eisler, *The Chalice and the Blade* (San Francisco, CA: Harper & Row, 1988), 72.

10. Herbert Silberer, *Hidden Symbolism of Alchemy and the Occult Arts* (New York, NY: Dover Publications, 1971; originally published in Germany in 1914), 399.

11. Richard Webster, *Write Your Own Magic* (St. Paul, MN: Llewellyn Publications, 2001), 150–155.

Chapter Six

1. Richard Webster, *Aura Reading for Beginners* (St. Paul, MN: Llewellyn Publications, 1996).

Chapter Seven

1. Exodus 30:1, 30:27–34, 37:29, Leviticus 2:1–10, 10:1, 16:13, Numbers 16:46, Luke 1:9.

2. I have found the following books helpful: *The Complete Book of Incense, Oils and Brews* by Scott Cunningham (St. Paul, MN: Llewellyn Publications, 1989), *Wylundt's Book of Incense* by Steven R. Smith (York Beach, ME: Samuel Weiser, Inc., 1989), and *Incense: Its Ritual Significance, Use, and Preparation* by Leo Vinci (Wellinborough, UK: Aquarian Press, 1980).

3. A range of mantras can be found in: *Write Your Own Magic* by Richard Webster (St. Paul, MN: Llewellyn Publications, 2001), and *Practicals of Mantras and Tantras* by L. R. Chawdhri (New Delhi, India: Sagar Publications, 1985).

4. Richard Webster, *Write Your Own Magic*, 106.

Chapter Eight

1. Camillus Leonardus, quoted in *History and Mystery of Precious Stones* by William Jones (London, UK: Richard Bentley and Son, 1880), 31.

2. Bruce G. Knuth, *Gems in Myth, Legend and Lore* (Thornton, CO: Jewelers Press, 1999), 77.

3. Damigeron, translated by Patricia P. Tahil, *De Virtutibus Lapidum: The Virtues of Stones* (Seattle, WA: Ars Obscura, 1989), 14.

4. William Jones, *History and Mystery of Precious Stones*, 35.

5. Andreas, quoted in *The Curious Lore of Precious Stones* by George Frederick Kunz (New York, NY: J. B. Lippincott Company, 1913), 311–312.

6. Camillus Leonardus, *The Mirror of Stones: In Which the Nature, Generation, Properties, Virtues and Various Species of more than 200 Different Jewels, Precious and Rare Stones are Distinctly Described.* (London, UK: J. Freeman, 1750), 228. (Originally published as *Speculum Lapidum* [Venice, Italy, 1502].)

7. George Frederick Kunz, *The Curious Lore of Precious Stones*, 59.

8. John Sinkankis, *Emerald and Other Beryls* (Prescott, AZ: Geoscience Press, 1989), 73.

9. Reginald Scot, *The Discoverie of Witchcraft.* (Originally published in 1584, many editions available; the one I have was published by John Rodker, London, 1930), 124.

10. William Jones, *History and Mystery of Precious Stones*, 31.

11. Bartolomaeus Anglicus, quoted in George Frederick Kunz, *The Curious Lore of Precious Stones,* 105.

12. Onomacritis, quoted in *Precious Stones and Gems* by Edwin W. Streeter (London, UK: Chapman and Hall Limited, 1877), 17.

Chapter Nine

1. Richard Webster, *Aura Reading for Beginners* (St. Paul, MN: Llewellyn Publications, 1998), Mark Smith, *Auras: See Them in Sixty Seconds* (St. Paul, MN: Llewellyn Publications, 1997), and John Mann and Lar Short, *The Body of Light: History and Practical Techniques for Awakening Your Subtle Body* (Rutland, VT: Charles E. Tuttle Company, Inc., 1990) all contain methods for seeing auras.

2. Teilhard de Chardin, *Hymn of the Universe* (London: William Collins, 1959).

3. These two quotes are from the Revised Standard Version of the Bible. I have used it because in the Authorized Version the word "charity" is used instead of "love." It means the same thing, but for the purposes of this book the RSV version is clearer. Every other biblical quote in this book is from the Authorized Version.

4. Daya Sarai Chocron, *Healing the Heart: Opening and Healing the Heart with Crystals and Gemstones* (York Beach, ME: Samuel Weiser, Inc., 1989), 13.

Chapter Ten

1. C. G. Jung, *Memories, Dreams, Reflections* (London, UK: Collins and Routledge & Kegan Paul, 1963), 308.

Chapter Eleven

1. Richard Webster, *Spirit Guides and Angel Guardians* (St. Paul, MN: Llewellyn Publications, 1998), 50–58.

Suggested Reading

Apocrypha: The Books Called Apocrypha According to the Authorized Version. London, UK: Oxford University Press, n.d.

Black, Matthew (commentator and editor). *The Book of Enoch or 1 Enoch: A New English Edition.* Leiden, Netherlands, 1985.

Brandon, S. G. F. *Religion in Ancient History.* London, UK: George Allen and Unwin Limited, 1973.

Brockington, L. H. *A Critical Introduction to the Apocrypha.* London, UK: Gerald Duckworth and Company Limited, 1961.

Bunson, Matthew. *Angels A to Z.* New York, NY: Crown Trade Paperbacks, 1996.

Burnham, Sophy. *A Book of Angels: Reflections on Angels Past and Present and True Stories of How They Touch Our Lives*. New York, NY: Ballantine Books, 1990.

Cahill, Thomas. *Desire of the Everlasting Hills*. New York, NY: Nan A. Talese, division of Doubleday Dell Publishing Group, Inc., 1999.

Connell, Janice T. *Angel Power*. New York, NY: Ballantine Books, 1995.

Daley, Brian E. *The Hope of the Early Church: A Handbook of Patristic Eschatology*. Cambridge, UK: Cambridge University Press, 1991.

Davidson, Gustav. *A Dictionary of Angels*. New York, NY: The Free Press, 1967.

Fox, Matthew and Sheldrake, Rupert. *The Physics of Angels: Exploring the Realm Where Science and Spirit Meet*. San Francisco, CA: HarperSanFrancisco, 1996.

Ginzberg, Louis (translated by Henrietta Szold). *The Legends of the Jews*, 7 volumes. Philadelphia, PA: The Jewish Publication Society of America, 1909- 1937.

Giovetti, Paola (translated by Toby McCormick). *Angels: The Role of Celestial Guardians and Beings of Light*. York Beach, ME: Samuel Weiser, Inc.,1993.

Hodson, Geoffrey. *The Angelic Hosts*. London, UK: The Theosophical Publishing House Limited, 1928.

Jones, Timothy. *Celebration of Angels*. Nashville, TN: Thomas Nelson Publishers, 1994.

Lippman, Deborah and Colin, Paul. *How to Make Amulets, Charms and Talismans: What They Mean & How to Use Them.* New York, NY: M. Evans and Company, Inc., 1974.

Milik, J. T. (editor). *The Books of Enoch: Aramaic Fragments of Qumrân Cave 4.* Oxford, UK: Oxford University Press, 1976.

Muhammad, Shaykh and Kabbani, Hisham. *Angels Unveiled: A Sufi Perspective.* Chicago, IL: Kazi Publications, Inc., 1995.

Myer, Isaac. *Qabbalah, the Philosophical Writings of Solomon Ben Yehudah Ibn Gebirol or Avicebron.* London, UK: Robinson and Watkins, 1972. (First published in Philadelphia, 1888.)

Parrinder, Geoffrey. *Worship in the World's Religions.* London, UK: Faber and Faber Limited, 1961.

Pseudo-Dionysius (translated by Colm Luibheid). *Pseudo-Dionysius: The Complete Works.* Mahwah, N.J.: Paulist Press, 1987.

RavenWolf, Silver. *Angels: Companions in Magic.* St. Paul, MN: Llewellyn Publications, 1996.

Ringgren, Helmer (translated by David Green). *Israelite Religion.* London, UK: S.P.C.K., 1966.

Schneider, Petra and Pieroth, Gerhard K. *Archangels and Earthangels: An Inspiring Handbook on Spiritual Helpers in the Metaphysical and Earthly Spheres.* Twin Lakes, WI: Arcana Publishing, 2000.

Schouten, J. *The Pentagram as a Medical Symbol*. Nieuwkoop, Netherlands: De Graaf, 1968.

Shinners, John (editor). *Medieval Popular Religion 1000–1500: A Reader*. Peterborough, Canada: Broadview Press, 1997.

Swedenborg, Emmanuel. (translated by George F. Dole). *Heaven and Hell*. West Chester, PA: Swedenborg Foundation, 1976.

Sweetman, J. Windrow. *Islam and Christian Theology*, 4 volumes. London, UK: Lutterworth Press, 1947.

Webster, Richard. *Spirit Guides and Angel Guardians*. St. Paul, MN: Llewellyn Publications, 1998.

Welburn, Andrew. *Mani, the Angel and the Column of Glory: An Anthology of Manichaean Texts*. Edinburgh, Scotland, 1998.

Index

Aaron, 107, 115

Abraham, 1

addiction, 18–19, 110

affirmations, xiii, 99–102, 104, 119

Agrippa, Cornelius, 53

air, 9, 11, 15, 22, 25, 33, 54–55, 57, 60, 62, 67–68, 70, 82, 85, 87–88, 90, 94–97, 100, 104–105, 133

Alexander the Great, 110

Allah, 95

altar, 22–23, 25–26, 108

amber, 113, 124

amulets, 46–47, 51–53, 66, 111, 115, 121

angelite, 108

Anglicus, Bartolomaeus, 116

Antiochus, 53

Apocrypha, 2

Aquinas, Thomas, xii, xv
Aristotle, 111
Asmodeus, 3–4
auras, 78, 80–81, 122–123, 132
aventurine, 46, 109, 125
Azarias, 3–5

Babylon, 52, 90, 111
Bede, the Venerable, xvii
Beelzebub, 7
beryl, 111, 114–115
Bethesda, 8
Bible, xv, 6, 90, 96, 107
blue, 46, 56, 64, 79, 81, 108, 112, 125–126, 132
Booth, William, xv
Botticelli, 11
breath, 15, 29, 50, 76, 82, 88–89, 103, 136–137

Caedmon, xvii
candle, 22–23, 27, 54, 56–57, 66, 94
Capernaum, 52
carnelian, 115, 124
celestite, 108
chakras, 122–138, 146–147
Chamuel, 124
chanting, 95, 101
de Chardin, Teilhard, 135
chrysoprase, 110
citrine, 115, 125
cleansing, 91, 108–109, 134
Cleopatra, 111

color, 23, 29, 78–81, 89, 109, 111–113, 123–128, 131, 133, 146

color breathing, 29, 79–81, 127

confidence, xviii, 28–29, 36, 40, 67, 81, 91, 109, 112, 115, 119, 134

creativity, xix, 11, 32, 34, 40, 45–46, 105, 113, 124–126, 138–147

crystals, 22, 46, 68–70, 107–109, 114, 116, 118–119, 121–122, 124–127

Damigeron, 111

darts, 104–106

Delphi, 90

diamond, 116–117

Diodorus Siculus, 54

divination, 91, 114

doodles, 30–33

dowsing, 119, 121

dreams, xvi, 32, 41, 43, 91, 102, 111, 115–116, 121, 149

Dwaraka, 107

earth, xii, xvi, 1, 5, 9, 22, 25, 48, 51, 54–55, 57, 59, 64, 68, 87, 94, 98, 109, 131, 137

Eckhart, Meister, xv

Egypt, 4, 90, 111

Egyptian *Book of the Dead,* 115

emerald, 111–112, 125, 133

Enoch, xvi, 2, 5–7

Feast of the Archangels, 12

fire, 22, 25, 54–55, 57, 62–63, 66–67, 87–88, 94, 135

Francis of Assisi, Saint, xvi, 24–25
frankincense, 90–93

Gabriel, xix, 5–6, 12, 23, 25–27, 61, 63–65, 95, 126
Galen, Claudius, 112
gemstones, 106–109, 113–114, 116–117
glossolalia, 98
Golden Dawn, 58
golem, 94
Gouda Surgeon's Guild, 53
green, 23–24, 29, 46, 64, 70, 79, 89, 108–109, 111–112, 125, 131, 133, 135, 138
Gregorian chant, 95

healing, xi–xii, xix, 1, 5, 11, 15–16, 22–23, 27–28, 31, 34, 37–38, 45–46, 48–49, 52, 57, 59, 70, 72–79, 81–85, 89, 91, 107–109, 111, 113, 116–117, 122, 128, 135
  absent, 84
  emotional, 1, 11, 16, 38, 45, 73, 110
heart, xv, 3–4, 59, 74, 82, 103, 113, 125, 128–138, 146–147
herbs, 90, 94
Hermas, 1
hexagram, 66, 71
Hildegarde, Saint, 117
Holy Grail, 110

incense, 4, 22–23, 90, 93–94
indigo, 79–80, 126
insufflation, 89
intuition, 79, 91, 126
Islam, 95

Jacob, 1
jade, 111–112, 125
jasper, 112, 124–125
Jesus, xiii, 11, 54, 78, 132, 138
John, Saint, xii, 107, 110
Jung, Carl, 143

Koran, xv, 95, 107
Krishna, Lord, 107
kyphi, 90

learning, xii, 8, 13, 30, 45–46, 89, 113, 142
Leonardus, Camillus, 110, 113, 116
Lorraine, Claude, 11
love, 9, 11, 24–27, 38, 40, 45, 48, 75–76, 79–80, 83–84, 89, 91, 111–112, 114–116, 118, 125, 128–138, 141
Lucian, 52

Magnus, Albertus, 110
Maimonides, Moses, xv
mandalas, 143–144
mantras, 95, 97, 102–104
Marissa, 52
meditation, 21, 24, 40, 48–49, 88, 92–94, 102, 104, 120, 133–135, 143
Mercury, 11, 13, 35, 67, 105
Metatron, xvi
Michael, 5–7, 12, 23, 25–27, 60, 62, 64–65, 77, 125
Milton, John, 8–10
Muhammad, 94, 115
myrrh, 90, 92–93

negativity, 54, 56–59, 83, 88, 99–100, 108, 111, 114–115,
      120, 128–129, 148
Nephilim, 6
Nicias, 113
Noah, 6–7

Onomacritis, 116
orange, 79, 87, 91–92, 113, 124
Ornias, 7
Oropel, 8

peace, 15–16, 24, 26–27, 35, 39, 49–50, 67, 76, 79–80, 92,
      103, 109, 133, 135
pendulum, 114, 119–121, 127
pentagram, 7, 50–56, 58–66, 71
philosopher's stone, 67
Plato, 73
Polo, Marco, 117
potpourri, 94
prayer, xiii, 2–3, 5–7, 24, 28, 47, 54, 90, 97, 104, 114, 116,
      119, 138
prosperity, 67, 92–93, 115
protection, xv–xvi, xviii, 25–26, 32, 35, 46, 49, 51, 53,
      55–61, 64, 66, 68–71, 91–92, 111, 114–116
Pseudepigrapha, 7
Puranas, 107
purification, 26, 58, 70, 92, 111, 114, 117
Pythagoras, 52

quartz, 46, 108–109, 116–117, 126

rainbow meditation, 127, 135

Ramiel, 12

red, 18, 63, 79, 81, 89, 112, 124

Rembrandt, 11

ritual, 12, 21–31, 33–34, 38–39, 46, 55–59, 61–62, 64–65, 68–71, 77, 136

  banishing, 58–59, 61, 64–65

  invoking, 58, 62

sacred space, 22–24, 29, 49, 59, 72, 91, 98, 101, 108, 120

Salvation Army, xv

Sandalphon, 124

sapphire, 116

Sariel, 5

Saxo, Arnoldus, 114

Scot, Sir Reginald, 114

Seal of Solomon, 66

selenite, 108, 126

Sennacherib, King, 2

Sermon on the Mount, 138

Shakti, 66

Shiva, 66

Solomon, 7–8, 50–51, 53, 66

spirituality, 93, 126

success, 28, 32, 93, 108, 111, 150

Swedenborg, Emmanuel, xv

Talmud, 107

Tarot cards, 22

Titian, 11

Tobias, 2–5, 9–11
Tobit, 2–5, 8, 10, 35
toning, 95

Uriel, 5, 24–27, 61, 64–65, 125

violet, 23, 80, 87, 92, 126, 128, 146
visualization, 19, 26, 29, 34–36, 49, 55–56, 58–59, 62, 64, 68–70, 75, 80, 82–83, 89, 93, 118, 127–128, 132, 136–138

Watchers, 5–6
water, 8, 10, 22, 25, 31, 35, 54–55, 57, 63–64, 67, 87, 94, 109, 113–114, 119
Whittier, John Greenleaf, xvii
wholeness, xix, 11, 14, 32, 34, 68, 70–71, 148
wind, 33–34, 88, 97
wind chimes, 97
wisdom, xii, 93, 126, 150

yellow, 23, 35, 46, 62, 79, 108, 112–113, 116, 125
yoga, 104

Zadkiel, 126

Free Catalog

Get the latest information on our body, mind, and spirit products! To receive a **free** copy of Llewellyn's consumer catalog, *New Worlds of Mind & Spirit,* simply call 1-877-NEW-WRLD or visit our website at www.llewellyn.com and click on *New Worlds.*

LLEWELLYN ORDERING INFORMATION

Order Online:
Visit our website at www.llewellyn.com, select your books, and order them on our secure server.

Order by Phone:
- Call toll-free within the U.S. at 1-877-NEW-WRLD (1-877-639-9753). Call toll-free within Canada at 1-866-NEW-WRLD (1-866-639-9753)
- We accept VISA, MasterCard, and American Express

Order by Mail:
Send the full price of your order (MN residents add 6.5% sales tax) in U.S. funds, plus postage & handling to:

Llewellyn Worldwide
2143 Wooddale Drive, Dept. 978-0-7387-0649-8
Woodbury, MN 55125-2989

Postage & Handling:

Standard (U.S., Mexico, & Canada). If your order is:
$24.99 and under, add $3.00
$25.00 and over, FREE STANDARD SHIPPING

AK, HI, PR: $15.00 for one book plus $1.00 for each additional book.

International Orders (airmail only):
$16.00 for one book plus $3.00 for each additional book

Orders are processed within 2 business days.
Please allow for normal shipping time. Postage and handling rates subject to change.